From the Ground Up

BY GOODWIN STEINBERG, F. A. I. A.

with Susan Wolfe

From the

STANFORD UNIVERSITY PRESS ■ STANFORD, CALIFORNIA 2002

Ground Up

BUILDING SILICON VALLEY

Stanford University Press
Stanford, California

© 2002 by the Board of Trustees of the Leland Stanford Junior University.

Printed in the United States of America on acid-free, archival-quality paper.

Library of Congress Cataloging-in-Publication Data

Steinberg, Goodwin B.
From the ground up : building Silicon Valley / by Goodwin B. Steinberg with Susan Wolfe.
   p. cm.
ISBN 0-8047-4529-3 (alk. paper)
   1. Architecture—California—Santa Clara Valley (Santa Clara County)—20th century
2. Regional planning—California—Santa Clara Valley (Santa Clara County)   3. Santa Clara Valley (Santa Clara County, Calif)—History.   I. Wolfe, Susan, 1959–   II. Title.
NA730.C22 S268   2002
720'.92—dc21

2002004725

Original Printing 2002
Last figure below indicates year of this printing:
11   10   09   08   07   06   05   04   03   02

Designed by Janet Wood
Typeset by Janet Wood and James P. Brommer in 11/14 Adobe Garamond

To Gerry, with love

Contents

My friend Goodwin Steinberg has regaled me on many occasions with stories of his interest in buildings and people. He aptly begins his autobiography with one of these vignettes from his youth. His father had given him a project to design a cemetery. Young Goody was told to "make it beautiful" and to consider the living as well as the dead. He plunged into the project with great enthusiasm. "I thought I was an architect at eleven years old," he writes. This story of his first introduction to design tells volumes about the man, and is a fitting beginning to a book that is a chronicle of a career and life well lived.

In the simplest terms, this is the autobiography of a man building his life as an architect of no mean accomplishments in the dynamic growth environment of California, and greatly enhancing our com-munity along the way. But the pages of this book are not merely about buildings, great and small; they are about the impulses that led people to California—and to our valley in particular—in the post–World War II population tilt. It is a very human and personal story, remarkable, as the author well knows, because of its com-monality. In telling his own story, he tells that of all who helped make our valley such a unique place.

This is a tale of one young ser-viceman and his bride, who came to a "Valley of Heart's Delight" and helped make it a place of legend and undreamed-of wealth. The son of an architect and a native of Chicago, one of many GIs among the thousands who got off the train in California, Steinberg arrived as a man in search of his future and a place to call home. In the beautiful Santa Clara Valley, Steinberg found a place worthy of his talent. His book captures the mystery and the vitality of this new place, as well as its potential. He shows how, in the years that followed, his success would be measured by many significant contributions to the look, feel, and economic health of our region.

But this is not just a series of descriptions of buildings and money and their interplay; it is the story of how dreams can come true if they are backed by fine ideas and hard work. It shows how one man can indeed make a difference, even in such a rarified atmosphere. Winston Churchill said that we shape our buildings and then they shape us. The contributions of Steinberg are inseparable from our community, from the mango-colored Tech Museum of Inno-vation and the functional and hard-won Children's Shelter for those most in need of succor to

Foreword

the vintage nineteenth-century courthouse at St. James Park and many parts of the stately campus of Stanford University. Along the way, his flair for building senior housing and the homes of Silicon Valley titans reveals much about his lifework. In all of these endeavors, you see Steinberg's interest in and talent for beautiful lines and public spaces and his concern for enjoyment and circulation, for allowing people to explore their surroundings.

As good as his work on buildings is, perhaps his finest hour was to play the key role of citizen adviser to the creation of the Guadalupe River Park, a long ribbon of watery green in the heart of San Jose. This project has been as challenging as it is spectacular. As it is now taking shape, its walks and public spaces—areas that could easily have been an afterthought—are as beautiful as any project anywhere, and the best is yet to come. Steinberg's vaunted teamwork concept and sound judgment, combined with San Jose Redevelopment Agency Director Frank Taylor's driving force, provided a rare symmetry to this grand public project. San Jose's rebirth as a place for families and children was ensured, as the book details, by the city's success in creating its walks, fountains, parks, and historical areas—all done with sensitivity and taste.

It is often said that art is a collaborative process, and much time in Steinberg's book is devoted to the ideas of teamwork and balance. Steinberg is particularly

good at working through the labyrinthine ways of government. I know this firsthand, and occasionally I have marveled as I watched his talent—and his diplomacy—as the coordinating architect at the Tech Museum, the defining building of our valley, which had to equal the majesty of the mountains of technology already here. In managing this project he balanced the creative force of a world-class architect, Ricardo Legoretta, the strong will and sound ideas of the downtown czar, Frank Taylor, as well as the input of two or three billionaires, who made for a few more lively chefs in the kitchen. The Tech Museum project became one cohesive implementation; Steinberg recognized that in Silicon Valley, you collaborate or you perish. You have only to visit Chavez Plaza in downtown San Jose to witness the success of this complicated but magnificent enterprise.

Working with government is a time-consuming and demanding skill for any architect—and definitely not for the faint of heart. There has been no better coordinator and collaborator in this field than Goodwin Steinberg. He knows well that although the political arm can be unpredictable, it must be vital and strong, able to weather ignorant criticism of good ideas or relentless parodying of poor ones. He also understands that the private side must be equally constant, forceful, and energetic. The balance between the public and private in these large projects is attained through

hard work and sound judgment. Such judgment has left a legacy of powerful projects as testimony to Steinberg's skill and unceasing commitment.

In the pages of this book we see what has transpired in the many years since that long train journey brought Steinberg to California. There is much to recall. This book's perspective is, of course, a personal one. Yet it is also a view of a valley that has changed so much, yet retains strong elements of what drew so many young people here in the first place. The author knows his era well, and whether his story is about designing a cathedral of technology or a home for children with a special need for love, Steinberg tells it with the same grace and gusto of the young GI who disembarked from that train in 1944. Although he has since participated in great endeavors, he has retained the common touch. Seldom, in examining his life's work, has anyone explored the convergence of talent and inspiration within the context of time and place as Steinberg does in *From the Ground Up*. This is the singular voice of a person who has seen our valley's evolution into the greatest economic engine in the history of the planet. That young boy from far-off Chicago has come a long way, and he has proved how much can be accomplished when you combine hard work and a dream.

The Hon. Tom McEnery
Mayor of San Jose, 1983–1990

Writing *From the Ground Up: Building Silicon Valley* has been a labor of love. It has allowed me the opportunity to recollect and reconnect with friends and colleagues I have known through the years as I revisited projects long since completed and tested out my hypotheses on why Silicon Valley developed the way that it did.

I am especially grateful to Frank Taylor and Ken Talbot for the knowledge I gained while working with them and the San Jose Redevelopment Agency. My good friend Tom McEnery also contributed to my on-the-job education in urban planning. During development of the manuscript, he provided a reliable reality check for me and graciously agreed to write the book's Foreword.

My thanks also go to the many friends, clients, and colleagues who recalled with me and shared their perspectives on regional planning. I note particularly the conversations I had with Larry Livingston, Dianne McKenna, Rebecca Morgan, Susan Hammer, Larry Dawson, Don Seiler, David House, Robert Fenwick, Mervin Morris, Lindley Miller, Robert Huff, and Elliott Levinthal.

Charlotte Siegel, Leigh Weimers, and Bill Pattis helped to get the project off the ground when it was but a pipe dream. As it progressed, Frederic Stout, David Neuman, Richard Lyman (the former president of Stanford University), and especially Norris Pope at Stanford University Press provided valuable editorial guidance and insights.

Special thanks to my good friend Susan Wolfe, whose patience, attention to detail, and support have made writing this book a total pleasure. Her graceful way with words enriches and enlivens my stories; her sense of flow and structure helped to produce a cohesive narrative.

I appreciate so much the help of Robert Steinberg, Denise Youmans, Tina Lee, Araceli Arreola, and Jodi Mulcahy of The Steinberg Group, whose diligence in tracking down photographs and floor plans made possible the inclusion of graphics to support and reinforce the text.

My daughter, Joanie, and my wife, Gerry, carefully read the evolving manuscript and offered helpful suggestions along the way. Gerry's painstaking attention to every detail helped me to produce a manuscript that I am proud of.

I especially thank Gerry for her patience, not only while the book was in progress, but throughout our more than fifty years together.

Acknowledgments

If it hadn't been for Grand Island, Nebraska, I might never have made the Bay Area my home.

In 1944, I was a corporal serving in the United States Air Force. My brand-new wife and I had been sent to Grand Island, where I was engaged in military intelligence. It was a railroad town, barren and sparse, where acre after acre of level farmland melted into the horizon. In June, the weather was hot, dry, and uncomfortable. By December, the temperature had dipped to zero degrees—25 below zero with the windchill factor—and even though we were born and bred in Chicago, where we had experienced cold before, we still were miserable in this harsh, frigid wasteland.

Imagine our joy at being boarded on a train bound for Oakland, California, transfer papers in hand. Destination: Hamilton Air Force Base in the Golden State's resplendent Marin County.

The trip took three long and tedious days. The train was stuffy and crowded. We did not sleep well. But when we arrived in Oakland, disheveled, tired, hungry, and spent, we felt as though we had stepped into Shangri-la. The late afternoon sun bathed our faces; the winter temperature seemed almost tropical at 55 degrees. By bus we crossed the Golden Gate Bridge, marveling at the sparkle of San Francisco Bay as the sun set over the Pacific Ocean. Large plate-glass windows on houses dotting the surrounding hills of San Francisco, Sausalito, and Tiburon reflected the day's rays. Both my bride and I were overwhelmed by the beauty.

With five days' leave before reporting for duty, we played tourist in San Francisco and environs, eating our way through Chinatown, Fisherman's Wharf, and North Beach; touring the vista points of Belvedere, Tiburon, and Mill Valley; marveling at the varied architectural styles, from Victorians in the city to Marin County houseboats with views of Angel Island and the island prison of Alcatraz. As an aspiring architect, I thought to myself, "Designing buildings here would be a dream. There's no place in the world compared to this."

Eight years and two children later, we finally made our way back to the Bay Area, to make the South Peninsula town of Los Altos our home. By then, I had received my architectural degree from the University of Illinois. In addition to learning about function, engineering, and refinement of design, I had also developed a special sensitivity to mood, recognizing

Just after we were married in 1944, Gerry and I spent six months in Grand Island, Nebraska, where I served in the United States Air Force. From there, I was sent to Hamilton Air Force Base in Marin County, and then to Tinian Island in the Pacific. After the war, thousands of GIs who had passed through the Bay Area just as I had on their way to and from tours of duty in the Pacific returned there. To me, the San Francisco Bay Area presented an irresistible opportunity to build an architectural practice. More importantly, it seemed to me to be the perfect place to raise a family.

Prologue

that how people feel in a space significantly affects its function and comfort.

Architecture is a discipline of solving problems—a problem-and-solution game mixed with art and aesthetics, function and calculation, budget and time schedules. Working with a team that may include architects, engineers, consultants, clients, and government planners is tremendously satisfying. Many people pursue the challenge and satisfaction of problem-solving by spending their leisure time engaged in math or crossword puzzles, or playing chess; imagine how much more satisfying it is when the problem is multilayered, ranging from how to place a building on a site, to how to design for the specific business to be conducted inside it, to how to determine the function and fit of each room within the overall design and purpose. During my fifty-year career, I have found the process of working with a client's needs and desires, planning the solutions with a team, partnering with a contractor to execute the plan, and enjoying the final product to be richly rewarding. I am lucky to have found a profession so personally fulfilling.

This book describes in some detail the collaborative vision of those of us who found ourselves trying to build a life on the San Francisco Peninsula before it became the world-renowned Silicon Valley. In addition to the area's often cited expertise in business, law, and finance, the thought given to

regional planning by urban planners, architects, real estate professionals, and the hundreds of thousands of newcomers anxious to build a life in cooperation with one another helped to ensure that the Santa Clara Valley would take measures to minimize urban sprawl. This was accomplished, for example, by implementing a green line around San Jose that limited development on the city outskirts, by enacting ordinances to limit development in the hills, and by benefiting from watchdog committees in the environmental movement. Though not perfect by any means, the cities within the county have managed extreme growth better than other areas such as Southern California, Florida, and Arizona. The sense of energy and momentum and the opportunity to participate in political leadership created the opening to build a great way of life in a beautiful and undeveloped area.

The synergy between land development and business growth helped to facilitate the region's success. And when environmentalists and urban planners became involved in the process, they urged us—sometimes coerced us—into building a region not only where business could flourish, but also where people would want to live. Soon the look and feel of business parks, government buildings, and even residential housing areas echoed a quality of life that especially valued open space, access to recreation, and attention to aesthetics. Communities, government

bodies, urban planners, architects, and real estate developers also worked together to address social problems. The expense and shortage of housing for low- to mid-salaried local workers and the need for better transportation are two areas that we continue to address together.

After thousands of architectural projects spanning a professional lifetime, here is a view of the conditions that I found when I came here and how we capitalized on them to build Silicon Valley.

Goodwin Steinberg, F.A.I.A.
Los Altos, California

From the Ground Up

I got my first design job when I was twelve.

My father came home from the office one day with a challenge: how to fit the greatest number of cemetery plots on a triangle-shaped property of rolling hills and meadows. An urban architect, my father worked mostly on industrial projects—hospitals, shopping centers, and industrial buildings—in downtown Chicago. Occasionally, he got a more unusual assignment, like the cemetery job that he brought home to me. This project, he said, would test my ability.

Today, a computer could solve my father's maximization project in an hour. But in the 1930s, when I was a boy, I worked for weeks, slotting plots into place as close together as possible and drawing, by hand, what I was sure must be the "right" solution. Each day after school I ran to my drafting board, neglecting my homework until I had finished my study of the layout of the cemetery plots. When, at last, I proudly presented my plan to my father, he smiled.

"That's very good, Goody," he said to me, "but how will the mourners get to the gravesides? We need to put roads in this cemetery, and walkways and benches where people can sit and remember those who have died. And there has to be enough space around each plot to conduct a funeral service.

"The cemetery has to be able to function," he said.

Then he reminded me that the financial success of the project depended on selling a maximum number of plots. We would have to lose some plots to roads and walkways and benches, but "not too many," my father sternly warned.

Back to the drafting board I went, somewhat sullen. I felt like I was starting all over again, like my weeks of work had gone to waste. Why hadn't he given me all the information at the outset?

I looked again at the triangular lot, the rolling hills with a creek on one side, and I considered how to use these features to my advantage. How could I make the roads curve in interesting ways without forfeiting too many gravesites? Facing another blank page of drafting paper, I set to work anew, retaining sections of my former plan but incorporating access ways and open spaces, as my father had told me to do.

Weeks later, I returned to my dad with a new plan—a plan with good circulation and good function and lots and lots of cemetery plots. (It looked pretty nice, too, if I say so myself.) With my dad's help, I had incorporated function and a little touch of design into my drawing, which initially was concerned only with economics.

1

"Hmmm," my dad pondered. "That's pretty darn good."

I felt so happy and proud.

But a moment later, he spoke again.

"Don't you think a few trees would be nice?" he asked.

Before I could answer, he continued, brainstorming aloud as if I weren't even there. "And some green belts with flowers, and maybe a planting strip with lacy-leafed trees in the middle of the road to separate the two-way traffic? Oh, and maybe, at the end of the road, as you come over this hill," he pointed to my plan, "you might find a little lake."

He looked up.

"What do you think, Goody? A cemetery shouldn't look like a desert, with only roads and graves, huh?"

As I headed back to the drawing board for the third time, my father called out, "But don't lose too many plots, or the project won't be built."

Now he had introduced me to the third element of architecture: design. Adding mood and feeling to economics and utility allowed me to create a cemetery that felt like a park. I worked faster now, eager to show off to my dad that I got it, that I finally understood what an architect does. After several days, I approached him again.

My father reviewed the drawings.

"I still think you can do better," he said.

Then he showed me a book on French palace gardens. It was filled with photographs of ponds and fountains and outdoor furniture. He said we needed some water features in our cemetery. We needed gates. We needed stonework and sculpture and benches.

"Go to the library and get some books," he said. "Look at Japanese gardens and English parks and European porches and patios," he said. "Study them. Make note of how you feel when you look at them. And then go back to your plan and see what you can do."

And then came the expected caveat. I could almost lip-synch it as he called out: "But don't forfeit too many plots!"

In the end, I felt great satisfaction. My father taught me to want it all— economic viability, practical function, and exquisite aesthetics—and to work hard not to sacrifice any of the three. It wasn't a matter of trade-offs, he said, it was a matter of balance, of taking the time to layer on each element and to do the best I could do. Though my father's client already had signed off on a plan that my father had drawn up himself, my finished cemetery was beautifully serene. It had places to sit and think, to converse and cry. Through environment and architecture, it conveyed to the people who found themselves there that someone had taken the time and care to create a quiet place for contemplation and an eternal resting place for their loved ones. I was proud of what I had learned and accomplished. At the age of twelve, I thought I was an architect.

Of course, it took years of training to become a real architect.

My parents sent me to a technical high school on the advice of my grammar school principal, who suggested that my dearth of academic ability equipped me well for a career in auto mechanics. But in addition to auto shop, Chicago's Lane Technical High School also offered classes in engineering and architecture. It was to these courses that I gravitated. The school's focus was technical: careful attention was given to design and construction, and I was blessed with talented teachers who instilled in me both an interest in math and a love for learning. At Lane, I learned how to draw in perspective, how to render with watercolor, how to work with shade and shadow, and how the sun affects the appearance and quality of life inside a building. Field trips took me and my classmates to construction sites, lumber mills, and sub-contracting shops, where we saw firsthand how cabinets are built, how glass becomes art, and how moldings are made. Through the field trips, I also gained an understanding of how an architect, a general contractor, and his sub-contractors work together to create a finished building.

After high school graduation, many of my classmates continued their architectural studies at the university level. I chose to attend the Illinois Institute of Technology, where the world-renowned German architect Ludwig Mies van der Rohe had just been hired to head the program. A leader of the Bauhaus movement, Mies's structural approach to architectural concepts focused on simplicity of design and attention to proportion. He considered decoration unnecessary: the hallmarks of clean architecture were structure, spacing, shade, and shadow. Under Mies's tutelage, I learned how to distill design down to its bare elements. To this day, I still reduce every one of my projects down to its essence, carefully considering choice of materials, construction details, underlying structure, and proportion in just the way that I learned at the Institute.

To understand Mies's approach, consider what might happen in two cities planning to build an important city hall, each with its own characteristic architecture. A local architect in Cape Cod might aim to recreate the colonial style of the city, using red brick with white wood trim, cobblestone entrances, white doors with traditional moldings, and rectangular mullions dividing the windowpanes. The building would take on the flair and personality of traditional Cape Cod architecture from all sides. Its decorative sculpture might be a steering wheel or an anchor from an old ship.

In Santa Fe, a city hall would more likely be made of tan adobe. Consistent with the mission architecture that characterizes the area, a sculpture meant to welcome the public might be a mission bell or tower from the local church—something that reflected the influence of the Southwest's mixed Spanish and Indian heritage.

Mies would have taken a very different approach. He had developed a style that reflected the machine age. It was dominated by steel and glass and often included marble or brick as infill for the walls. If Mies were hired to design a city hall, he would do so in his own style, whether the project was in New Mexico or Cape Cod—or Alaska or Mexico. The style would be Mies, not the style that defined the local community. Its details would reflect the study he had made on how steel meets glass or brick and how they weave together to form his architecture. It would be beautiful in its own way. But it would not attempt to be consistent with the character of the surrounding community.

To me, Mies reached perfection with his famous glass and steel high-rise buildings. His was a recognizable, signature style. I realized that if I wanted to make my own mark—which I did—I would have to take what I had learned from my celebrated professor and continue to develop my own style elsewhere.

My father had taught me to layer the seemingly competing interests of financial viability, utility, and aesthetics. Mies taught me the rudiments of design. The next step in my education was to learn how to solve problems of practicality.

The University of Illinois belonged to a group of architectural schools that promoted competition among students as the best learning laboratory. After a year at the Institute, I transferred to the university so I could compare my work not only with my own classmates' but also with that of architecture students across the country. Using the layering model my father had taught me early on, my first competition project consisted of a single room, solving for circulation and furniture placement and using ceiling height and window placement in order to vary the landscape views and exposure to sunlight. I was especially sensitive to the different moods achieved by changing the single element of ceiling height.

Once I had mastered a single room, the next project assignment was a series of rooms. I explored how multiple rooms related to one another and how people occupying them could achieve a sense of intimacy or an interactive experience as the mood struck them. Multiple-room projects grew into small building assignments: we learned to design exteriors and how to place buildings on flat lots or hills, orienting them for sun and shade. Adapting concepts and ideas developed by the renowned architects whose work we studied, we were able to solve design problems in unusual and often successful ways. The education soon progressed to more complicated projects, including multistory buildings, groups of structures, and land use planning.

Coursework at the University of Illinois included color, materials, and textures, as well as the nitty-gritty of mechanical, electrical, and plumbing systems. Different faculty members taught different theories, forcing each student to formulate his own vision and philosophy. This was quite a departure from the Institute, where Mies was the master and the students simply followed his lead.

Graduation from the University of Illinois was not the end of my education. After finishing architecture school, I was accepted into a fine arts program for American students at the Palace of Fontainebleau in France. Master classes for pianists, vocalists, and art students were offered, as well as an architecture program headed by Jean Labatut, a Frenchman who chaired Princeton University's program in architecture. For a Midwesterner with a limited education in music (two weeks with a piano teacher before I quit!), sitting on a palace patio hearing master classes in Mozart as the sun was setting on one of the palace's many lakes was not just an architectural education; it was a fine arts experience that sensitized my soul.

I learned many lessons that summer in France, from celebrity architects like Auguste Perret and Le Corbusier as well as from Professor Labatut.

Le Corbusier was an artist, a sculptor, and an architect, and his buildings had the flair of the European artist and sculptor of the 1950s. He brought color into his buildings with tile; he brought shape into his buildings with free-form sculpture; he would raise a building onto concrete columns and reveal a park-like setting underneath and within the building. We saw historical and modern buildings in unique European settings, including the palace at Versailles. Taking a critical look at big indoor spaces as well as large and small gardens helped me to get a feeling for the kind of space that best accommodates a given number of people. This was very helpful as I took on projects that included plazas, sporting arenas, and traffic circulation.

All these experiences and interactions advanced my education, but from Labatut I learned a lesson that has informed my entire architectural career: how people feel in a space significantly affects its function and comfort.

During that summer, Labatut invited several of us to dinner at one of his favorite restaurants. It was evening; the sun had set. Lit only by candles, you could hardly see the inside of the building, only the candlelight dancing on people's faces. The delicious aroma, the violin music, the relaxation that wine provided all contributed to the mood for our little dinner.

"Is this good architecture?" Labatut leaned over and asked me.

I looked around. I could not see the ceiling, the walls, nor the details of décor; I could see only candlelight reflected in wineglasses and contented diners' smiling eyes. In that moment, I understood the extra dimension, the appeal to the senses that was so important to good architecture. It is a lesson that I have tried to carry into my work as an architect over the past fifty years, and it influences the way I look at the region that has come to be known as Silicon Valley.

But I was not to head west to the Bay Area just yet. Two detours would ultimately lead to the decision to move to the Santa Clara Valley. One was working for my father; the other was working for my father-in-law. Though I learned a great deal from each of them, what I learned most of all was that I would find it difficult working for anyone but myself.

My father's architecture practice was heavily influenced by the Depression. In order to work in his field during this period, he capitalized on the opportunity to remodel and add to existing industrial buildings outside the city center of Chicago. With that background, he was able to develop a successful practice of inner-city industrial work that consisted of solving functional problems on tight budgets, with less emphasis on strong design.

Working with my father, I built on my university education by learning how to solve circulation problems and gaining a working understanding of mechanical and electrical systems. Efficiency experts showed me the benefit of detailed industrial engineering, but the practice did not have much of the fun stuff I learned in school. While my father viewed himself as a problem solver, I naively considered myself a designer.

It was a clash between these two views that ultimately led me impulsively to quit the firm.

We had contracted to provide plans to expand a ladies' washroom at a large printing plant. My dad was leaving town for two days; he asked me to draw up the expansion plans, which he would present to the client the morning of his return. The printing plant washrooms were standardized and functional, and my father left me many examples to follow, so the job was not at all complicated. But as I considered the ladies who used the washroom, I thought they might appreciate a washroom in which they could not only clean up but also check their hair or apply some lipstick. Instead of using the basic industrial fixtures and my dad's sample blueprints, I drew up plans that called for individual vanities with built-in washbasins and mirrors surrounded by lights. The effect resembled a movie star's dressing room. I was especially pleased that I could accomplish these upgraded aesthetics within the budget allocated for the project.

When my father returned, he glanced at the plans before heading off to meet with the client. He was livid.

"Damn it, Goody!" he yelled at me. "You just don't understand the problem! It's not how beautiful you make it, it's how you bolt the faucets to the basins so they don't get stolen!"

With that, I exploded and decided to leave.

In hindsight, I realize my father was right: I did not understand the problem. After a long working shift, these women only wanted to get home to their families. Industrial soap and commercial washing facilities allowed them to clean up and leave the plant quickly. They also allowed for minimal upkeep. I had not thought about how to keep the mirrors, light bulbs, and countertops clean and functioning with repeated use. I had been thinking only of aesthetics.

Not long after I left my father's practice, my father-in-law approached me. He had two daughters, no sons, and a very successful dress manufacturing business. His plant manufactured two lines: one for women and one for juniors. Four times a year—winter, spring, summer, and fall—each line came out with fifty new sample dresses. Fifty salesmen covered territories all over the United States. With no son to take over the business, my father-in-law asked if I would join him—at double the salary I was earning in architecture, and with the promise that one day I would be head of the company.

"It's similar to architecture," he told me. "There's design and color and fabrics. I think you'll love it just as much as I do."

My father-in-law was partially right: dress designers are artistic and creative. They have great sensitivity to color and texture and often use unusual combinations of fabrics, buttons, and jewelry. But the dress business is about fashion, which is very different than construction. In fashion, trends shift from year to year, sometimes season to season. One year, the hemlines are short; the next year, they are long. One year, the color green is all the rage; the next year, green is woefully passé. Construction, on the other hand, is a longer-term proposition, and as a result, its professionals approach their work with concern for lasting impact on both design and durability.

My experience in the fashion world taught me that it is the rough-and-tumble construction worker, the thoughtful and meticulous structural engineer, and the landscape architect concerned with environment who stimulate my thinking and make me happy to get up and go to work in the morning. Within two years of working in the dress company, I realized that I had to forfeit this fabulous financial opportunity for a more personally fulfilling career—in architecture.

If we stayed in Chicago, both my father and my father-in-law would be looking over my shoulder, second-guessing every move. But the idea of leaving the security of family and financial stability did not come easily to my wife, and even I had my doubts from time to time as we mulled over the decision to move to California with two small children and no job. It was as much an effort to convince myself as it was an attempt to persuade my wife when I assured her, "I know that we will make a living. Trust me."

A final hurdle to my wife's agonizing decision to leave the security of a loving family, who had given her every material thing she could want, and to leave friends who were still trying to persuade us to stay, was the idea of selling our home in Glencoe, Illinois. Gerry grew up as one of two sisters whose father adored them and gave them an all-embracing love and every possible material advantage, including tuition for a private girls' high school and Vassar College. Gerry found herself caught between an extremely successful and attentive father and a young, strong-willed husband.

After much emotional struggle, she agreed with me that moving was the right thing for us to do, and we put our house up for sale. After four long weeks on the market, our house finally had one offer at considerably lower than the asking price.

The buyer of our home knew that we were anxious to leave. Our family and friends were pressuring us to stay. As the date to close the sale neared, the buyer initiated a series of stalling tactics that delayed our move and heightened our anxiety. Our attorney advised us that the buyer's ulterior motive was to lower the sales price even further. He suggested we give him a closing deadline, after which the house would go back on the market.

With only one offer in four weeks at a rock-bottom price, I was hesitant to take a hard-line stance. We waited another week and a half. The sale did not close. Knowing the risk, I mustered my courage, peppered with anger, and called the buyer directly. "We close by 2 P.M. tomorrow or the house goes back up for sale," I told him.

At 2 P.M. the next day, the deal was sealed. We said our good-byes, loaded our two toddlers in the back seat of our coupe, and in the summer of 1952 we headed for California.

Like so many other post-war GIs, I was drawn to the memory of the San Francisco Bay Area I had visited while in the service as I pondered where to establish my career. Drawn by the beauty of the bay itself, by majestic spans that bridged land to land, by the solid mooring of the already bustling city of San Francisco, many veterans who had passed through on tours of duty were determined to return after the war. The city's appealing mix was a draw: from Fisherman's Wharf to Chinatown, from the financial district to clustered and well-defined residential neighborhoods, San Francisco was anchored in a way that some other large West Coast cities were not. It offered mature cultural amenities, from symphony to ballet to opera, and an established financial center. Full of energy and enthusiasm, we 1949 "49ers" had a range of choices of where to live: in the city itself or in one of its neighboring communities.

Marin County was magnificent. Open hillsides offered prime opportunities for a residential architect looking to open a practice. But the Golden Gate Bridge cut it off from the main north-south traffic artery between San Francisco and Los Angeles, and the hilly terrain and proximity to San Francisco meant that commercial development was unlikely there. An architect wanting to spread his wings beyond residential design would be limited in this beautiful but bedroom community.

The East Bay, too, had its advantages: the University of California at Berkeley offered intellectual and cultural amenities. But like Marin County, the communities of Walnut Creek, Orinda, Lafayette, and Moraga were primarily residential, servicing the hub of Oakland and housing commuters to San Francisco. Just as the Golden Gate Bridge separated Marin County from the main traffic route, the City of Oakland and the Bay Bridge separated the East Bay from San Francisco. The already high level of development around Oakland and its largely blue-collar population were also impediments to an aspiring architect. I saw greater opportunity in a less developed but more affluent area.

Then there was the San Francisco Peninsula, abundant in flat, open space, with good north-south traffic flow. It was home to an intellectual center that proved ripe for an ambitious architect seeking to invest himself in building a career. The temperate microclimate, generally ranging from 50 degrees in the winter to 90 degrees in the summer, was mild enough for outdoor sports, dining, and entertaining, while still variable enough to display seasonal changes: hillsides turning spring green to summer gold, autumn leaves, and sometimes even frost. Locked in by the bay on the one side and the Santa Cruz

2

Mountains on the other, the valley was largely protected from the high winds that sometimes plagued San Francisco.

Recreational and leisure opportunities were abundant, too, from Lake Tahoe and skiing to the east, to the Sacramento River Delta and water-skiing to the north, the Pacific Ocean to the west, and the restful Monterey Peninsula to the south.

Personalities also contributed to what came to be such a striking success story. We hear often of blue-jeaned inventors fashioning widgets in garages that somehow magically turn into a Varian Associates, a Hewlett-Packard, or an Apple Computer. But the atmosphere had long been uniquely risk-tolerant. After World War II, young veterans and their families came, without benefit of extended family, to take a chance on a new life in what was then uncharted territory. Their hunger to develop roots and their openness to new people, places, and ideas gave rise to the innovative spirit so strongly associated with Silicon Valley. Their businesses often were born in garages because they had no money to rent office space and their wives wanted them out of the house. With nowhere else to go, lawyers, accountants, and even architects set up shop with little more than a desk and a phone. Their courage, ingenuity, and innovation were instrumental in transforming the orchards of Santa Clara Valley into the high-tech hotbed since renamed Silicon Valley.

Stanford University, already well established at sixty years old, was the biggest enticement of all. In addition to being an intellectual and cultural center, the faculty demonstrated that a happy life could be lived on a modest income. As an architect with no job, striking out on my own with a young family to support, the Stanford faculty provided a model for living well. Substance was valued over style. Faculty wives were regarded as peers, fully involved in the concerns of the community. Friendships seemed likely; land was abundant and affordable. For many newcomers, these attractive elements constituted the makings of home.

Much has been written about the dazzling success story that is Silicon Valley—how and why high technology was fledged and flourished here, who the players were, and how the pieces came together. Influences ranging from San Francisco banking and financial communities seeking investment opportunities to the development of engineer-entrepreneurs at Stanford surely played major roles in the tidal wave of high technology so dominant in our world today. The interplay between science and business, between inquiry and incorporation, arose, no doubt, from the interdisciplinary model so prominent at major universities like Stanford in the post-war era.

Stanford cannot be underplayed as an important influence in the way that people in this valley thought and think now. As an emerging university of international renown, Stanford played an important role in bridging the gap between bench and business and in encouraging the growth of industry. Supported by strong regional institutions like San Jose State University and Santa Clara University, Stanford modeled an interdisciplinary way of approaching issues and challenges, combining business with law, for example, or medicine with engineering, or engineering with business.

Engineering Dean Frederick Terman is most often credited with establishing the interdisciplinary notion of engineer as entrepreneur. His reputation drew bright students, including many World War II veterans, from all over the country to train with professors and business people who were on the cutting edge in their fields. When they graduated, Terman wanted these students to remain in the area. It was important to him personally to establish the Santa Clara Valley as a region where engineer-entrepreneurs could prosper and build not only careers but also a way of life.

Just as they pursued their own careers and causes with passion, Stanford educators believed that their students ought to cultivate meaningful personal and professional interests. The faculty encouraged not only political, social, and cultural involvement, but also the study of subjects that students liked and knew and that would lead them to happy careers and happy lives. This lesson was especially apparent at the Stanford Design Conferences that the university's alumni association hosted each summer from 1976 to 1991. Open to students from colleges and universities nationwide and to the local community, these conferences illustrate the kind of cross-disciplinary thinking that was going on at Stanford and spilled over into the burgeoning valley.

Speakers came from all over the world to discuss their artistic pursuits at the design conferences. To me, the artistry was paramount, and a big draw. Although it might take me away from my work for two or three days, the opportunity to hear product designers, graphic designers, costume and clothing designers, filmmakers, photographers, color specialists, and architects discuss new solutions to existing problems held high appeal. The serenity of the Stanford campus was also rejuvenating: picnicking in natural oak groves, enjoying pastoral landscapes, and slowing the everyday workaday pace recharged a driven man's batteries. In combination with the discussions of functionality that students from the School of Engineering brought to the conference, attendees came away with a new appreciation for the balance between utility and aesthetics.

A memorable presentation of this balance came from an engineering student who loved the outdoors and hiking. He sought to design a more comfortable hiking boot. He pursued his research in an interdisciplinary way: he began at the medical center by asking, "What kinds of accidents, injuries, and ailments do hikers have?" There, he discovered that foot, ankle, knee, and hip problems are most common to avid hikers. In addition, he learned that many suffer from athlete's foot when moisture penetrates the shoe. Combining his interest in hiking with orthopedics, dermatology, and engineering, this student came up with a better and more aesthetically pleasing boot. It supported the bones in the foot and ankle, fit snugly, and contained materials watertight enough to protect the foot from outside moisture. It also had a tread pattern on the bottom to prevent slippage.

A second Stanford student cast a wide net in engineering a better way to photograph the stars. He studied the degrees of brightness in the night sky at different times of year, air density, and weather patterns to determine the most effective set-up spot. He surveyed film types and film development to determine which film products would produce the best pictures. And he looked at cameras—their lenses, sizes, and portability—to determine which tool was most suitable for -photographing the stars. Finally, he studied astronomy itself, to figure out which bodies—stars, planets, meteors, or asteroids—would make the best subject matter.

While Stanford students were engineering new and unusual products based on their personal interests and research, students who came to the design conferences from other universities most often were refining existing products. For example, a student from a large Midwestern university presented a study of a dashboard: how to illuminate it at night and where to place hand controls for the easiest access. His approach, based on studying hand-eye coordination, repeated a study that I had done years earlier as a student at the Illinois Institute of Technology. The creative, interdisciplinary thinking so clear in the Stanford-trained engineering students' demonstrations was not as evident in the projects presented by students from other schools.

Not every research project became a product for the marketplace, but Stanford wanted to help those students and faculty members whose ideas did merit commercial application. Besides the profit motive—Stanford was co–patent holder with many of its faculty inventors—the interest in facilitating its students' move from the academy to the marketplace was genuine. The overriding message to students was this: why go to work for someone else, when you can follow your passion and work for yourself?

With this as a mind set, change in the bucolic Valley of Heart's Delight was inevitable. In the 1950s, land to the south of Palo Alto was largely agricultural. The juiciest apricots and plums and cherries grew here. But with the influx of people and their business ventures and ideas, the farming community could not last. Government officials in the underdeveloped cities of Mountain View, Sunnyvale, Santa Clara, and Cupertino foresaw growth, and, fearing the sprawl of Southern California, they foresaw, too, the need for planning. Because it was further from San Francisco, property on the southern Peninsula was less expensive than it was to the north, and if attention were not paid to urban planning, that property was at risk of becoming a hodgepodge of strip malls, commercial buildings, and tract housing.

The region's growth and change appeared certain. So, knowing that they could neither freeze time nor stave off the unavoidable, civic leaders did what good parents do: they laid the foundation for a solid, well-balanced, and thoughtful coming-of-age. Then, having done the footwork, they watched, they waited, and they hoped for the best.

In addition to the young and ambitious people who came here, eager to build bright futures for themselves, there is another element, yet untold, that greatly influenced Silicon Valley history. That element is the land itself—its physical formation, its climate, its open spaces, and, most importantly, the forethought given to its development.

Abundant and inexpensive land offered newcomers to the Santa Clara Valley an opportunity that they could seize. Post-war GIs, Stanford graduates, and others attracted to the area could realize their dreams largely because they could afford to buy land—for their businesses, homes, and often in the early years, both.

Faced with the inevitable change that comes with an influx of people and a reputation for success, Santa Clara Valley government officials began to chart their futures. Would they become bedroom communities, industrial pockets, or a combination of both? Would they limit growth, or encourage it? The area was undeveloped and there were many choices.

Not surprisingly, there were a variety of opinions. Although there was a consensus to plan, several approaches emerged, from a big-city view of growth, to an idyllic, no-growth vision, to one that called for a balance between the extremes: moderate development and careful planning.

San Jose City Manager Anthony "Dutch" Hamann had a notion of how to grow the region *big*. The civic officials on the committee that had hired him wanted nothing less than to turn San Jose into the Los Angeles of the north, and Hamann and his staff worked relentlessly to achieve their vision. In the 1950s in San Jose, the city structure was such that the city manager held the power. Council members and mayors came and went; Hamann, who served as city manager from 1950 to 1969, called the shots. His crew aggressively sought out land parcels for annexation, going from farm to farm, badgering landowners until they agreed to part with their acreage. He made a science of snatching up bits of land whenever and wherever they became available. Over time, the city map took on the look of a giant octopus, with downtown San Jose at its center and tentacles stretching in all directions, weaving in and through neighboring cities' boundary lines.

A bit less highbrow than its neighboring cities, including Saratoga, Cupertino, and Los Gatos, the San Jose tentacles in the midst of the other cities allowed for higher-density housing, strip malls, and light industrial development among the custom homes of the more affluent cities. San Jose began to turn into a sprawl of one strip mall after another. There were so many cheap little shopping centers that the developers who built them had trouble leasing

3

the space; there was simply too much supply and not enough demand. Many of these little developments remained vacant, or soon became so, as merchants found a landlord who offered a lower rent in a similar building on a nearby corner. Boarded-up, often vandalized vacant properties resulted. This was one of the prices of Dutch Hamann's aggressive, pro-growth vision, and it strained relations between San Jose and its tonier neighbors.

But that was only one of the flaws of the octopus-shaped city. With the tentacles radiating so far out, it became difficult for San Jose to provide city services to all of the far-flung areas. Library branches varied greatly in quality; firefighters and police often took far too long to get to emergency sites because of the city's sprawl. Some raised the question of whether the annexations warranted the cost of providing such services, and the areas became somewhat neglected. The adjacent cities' leaders complained to San Jose Mayor Norm Mineta. So did the San Jose residents who lived in the outlying districts. But by that time, Mineta was already focused on a congressional seat and had little attention left for the city's political problems. Ultimately, Mineta became a congressman and cabinet member who served his constituents with enthusiasm and skill, leaving the challenge of the tentacled city to his successor.

When the University of California began looking for a new Northern California site to absorb the overflow from the perpetually overcrowded Berkeley campus, Hamann passionately wooed the site committee, hoping to attract them to the Almaden area of San Jose. He made a high-powered pitch for the campus, hoping to develop an environment like that of Westwood, which surrounds the University of California at Los Angeles. Had the site committee not fallen in love instead with the splendor of Santa Cruz, its green vistas and ocean views, tall trees and sunlit paths, San Jose might not have been as available for later development into Silicon Valley.

On the other side of the development issue, Santa Clara County's chief planner, Karl Belser, believed that, as he put it, "the Valley of Heart's Delight (was) going to hell in a hand basket." He believed that agriculture should be maintained as the primary industry and that it would afford residents a better quality of life than urban growth. His personal mission was to hold back the tidal wave of inevitable development. Whether behind the times, or ahead, Belser's vision was not realized any more than Hamann's was.

With multiple educational degrees and years of municipal and transit experience, attorney and urban planning consultant Larry Livingston took still another tack in the evolution of several South Peninsula communities, including Saratoga and the Town of Los Altos. Livingston's recommendations regarding planning issues, from open space and tree-planting programs to underground power lines and roads, helped city founders to make healthy long-term decisions for future quality of life. Town officials in Los Altos, which was incorporated in 1953, hired Livingston in 1954 to enter into a discussion of basic planning issues. What kind of community would they develop? How could the charm of Main Street be protected? What zoning was required to safeguard against strip malls? While Livingston advanced the vision, the civic leaders had the foresight to engage him and the perseverance to make the dream a reality.

An example of this fruitful collaboration lies in the way that Los Altos successfully managed to maintain the appeal of Main Street while expanding parking for increasing numbers of shoppers. Handed this challenge, Livingston came up with a novel idea. Noting the abundant open space that septic tanks had once occupied behind the storefronts, he proposed the concept of parking plazas, which are now in place not only in Los Altos, but also in Saratoga, Menlo Park, and other small-town downtowns. The idea was a winner, but making it happen was a venture of epic proportions. Merchants were asked not only to donate the valuable land they owned behind their stores to the city, but also to pay an assessment to pave and stripe that land, and purchase more land for parking.

A young real estate broker who was just starting in behind-the-scenes political work took the lead in convincing—and sometimes strong-arming—the merchants to move ahead with the plan. Alan Cranston had already made political points for himself when he revised the primary process to give Democrats an advantage in general elections. Democrats were indebted to him for that, and most of the merchants, it turns out, were Democrats. Cranston, who went on to become a United States senator, knew how to work the people and the process. Without his active participation and that of others like him, an outside consultant's ideas, however visionary, would never have become reality.

Savvy lawyers soon saw how government entities were seizing private land, not only in retail corridors but also in the more expansive agricultural areas. They devised ways to protect their agricultural clients, so much so that those who held out against selling to building interests, whether private or public, ultimately became the biggest winners financially. As time went on, and more and more land got bought up and developed, the remaining parcel owners garnered far more money per acre for their property than those who had responded to early pressures to sell. In 2000, only 4,515 acres of farmland remained in a valley that was once occupied by 106,115 acres of orchards and row crops.

Attorney Steven Nakashima was one such lawyer. He was adept at working the system to his clients' advantage. In the 1950s, the County of Santa Clara routinely was appropriating farmland for its own purposes—schools, government buildings, and the like—and a client of Nakashima's, a flower grower, became the target of such an eminent domain maneuver. Agricultural land was the cheapest to buy; land zoned for single-family dwellings was next, and by far the most expensive land was that zoned for multifamily dwellings and commercial use. Nakashima's flower grower fell into the agricultural category, of course, but with the help of an eager architect and a tax-hungry municipal government, the flower grower lost a profession but made a great profit.

Nakashima called me with a sense of urgency. He needed architectural drawings immediately for a multi-family residential development. Working round-the-clock, I delivered plans for a 400-unit apartment complex in a matter of days. With them, Nakashima approached the as yet unseasoned City of Mountain View, explaining that if the land could be rezoned and the residential development built, the city stood to gain a good deal in property tax revenue. The city took the bait. A rezoning process that now takes months and sometimes years was completed in a matter of weeks.

At the meeting that the county attorney called with Nakashima to discuss fair market value for the flower grower's land, out came a list of comparable agricultural properties and the relatively low prices paid to acquire them. When Nakashima brought out his paperwork indicating that the land under discussion was not agricultural but had been rezoned for multi-family residential use, the county attorney turned absolutely purple! That piece of paper increased the land price fivefold. Decades before technology tycoons became the stuff of Silicon Valley dreams come true, farmers and later developers were making their fortunes off the land.

Steve Vidovich belonged to a family of farmers who saw what developers were doing with farmland. Instead of selling, the Vidovich family decided to develop their Sunnyvale properties themselves. A draftsman who was leaving his job at my architectural firm presented Vidovich with some of my firm's ideas for a new home and won the contract to design one for Vidovich. Years later, Vidovich happened to see my firm's original plans, from which the design for his house was derived. He was so impressed that he decided to hire us to develop an office park for him. Vidovich became a major commercial developer, focusing on business parks and neighborhood shopping centers. Today, his son is carrying on, developing residential properties in the hills.

This type of development is part of the story of disappearing farmland all over the valley. Land speculators also sped the transformation of land use from agricultural to industrial. Rather than develop a site, land speculators "churned" the land, buying it for as little cash as possible, holding it, and selling it at significant profit a few years later.

For example, land speculator Warren Epstein was able to leverage a $100,000 down payment on a $1-million, 100-acre parcel into $3 million cash in just three years. His father, a principal in a San Francisco brokerage firm, had left him a small fortune to invest. Epstein hired a real estate agent, and together, they set out to find "spec" properties that could be had on a 10 percent down payment, held for a short time, and sold for significant gain.

The site at Bayshore and North First Street in San Jose was the most beautiful pear orchard in the valley. Epstein had the foresight to realize how strategically important this property would become. At the time, Bayshore was a four-lane highway; today it is a major freeway. North First Street was and is the main artery into downtown San Jose. Today, major high-rise hotels and upscale office centers occupy the former orchard, just outside the entrance to an expanding international airport.

Epstein knew that the acreage could not remain orchard for long. It was this parcel that he secured for 10 percent of the selling price and later sold for $3 million. Epstein went on to speculate on many other downtown San Jose land parcels.

In 1950, Silicon Valley was an undeveloped spread of agricultural land. Because of the hospitable climate, averaging from 50 degrees in the winter to 90 degrees in the summer, the area offered a wonderful lifestyle for people as well as ideal agricultural conditions, which produced the sweetest, juiciest cherries and the tastiest apricots.

Fifty years later, this same valley, developed to the maximum, has become a high-technology industrial center. It is the machine that pumps the nation's economy and provides much of the wealth that continues to make the United States the country with the highest quality of life in the world.

Silicon Valley developed differently than the hillsides and flatlands of Europe. In Europe, the flatland was reserved for agricultural use. It produced the food that sustained the population. Hillside land was not nearly as productive, and as a result, the hills in Europe were built up with houses, stores, and churches. The main disadvantage to hillside development is the substantially higher cost of construction. Transporting building materials up to the hillside sites is expensive; so is developing roads, water systems, and sewage systems.

In Silicon Valley, cost was the major factor in determining where to build. Industrial buildings that needed large, flat workspaces would not be fiscally feasible in the hills. As a result, agriculture was squeezed out and the flatlands became the main area of development, both for industry and housing.

To their credit, residents voted to tax themselves to buy open space, and they zoned the land to discourage development in the hills. The parks, hiking trails, and picnic areas woven through the hills surrounding Silicon Valley provide nearby recreational opportunities that improve the quality of life in an otherwise urban region.

Agricultural land was fast disappearing as it was developed for light industrial use. It appeared that a real estate investor couldn't lose. But timing is critical, and the market can change dramatically.

Not all speculators had the foresight and good fortune of Warren Epstein. A high-ranking Lockheed executive, for example, would have lost everything he had if he had not been as prominent in the business community as he was. This man had developer friends who, like Epstein, were cleaning up in real estate. Although he had a large salary, many stock options, and a wonderful home, he saw others succeeding in real estate and wanted a piece of that action as well. His personal assets were tied up in his Woodside home and in the opportunity to buy appreciating Lockheed stock at a locked-in lower price per share. But his reputation, combined with the leveraged value of his stock options, persuaded a bank to loan him a large sum for real estate investment purposes.

Having used his stock options as collateral to obtain a loan, the executive leveraged the dollars loaned him in real estate, as Epstein had, putting ten percent down and waiting for the property to appreciate. But at the time that he got the loan, the Lockheed stock was highly overvalued. After a market correction and a several-year dip in the economy, the bank realized that the value of the collateral stock no longer covered the amount loaned. Gun-shy after the economic downturn, the bank now wanted some repayment. But the executive had no money. All of his cash was tied up in real estate that also was depreciating. The executive became more and more nervous as, day after day, the value of his stock declined, the value of his land eroded, and the bank demanded more cash. Only because of his position at Lockheed was the executive able to delay bank foreclosure. Ultimately, the bank forced him to sell his spec property at a 25 percent loss and repay the rest of the loan in cash over time. Other less prominent speculators, developers, and contractors went bankrupt in just this way.

Another reason why farmers were leaving Santa Clara Valley was that land development—whether industrial or residential—was not compatible with the agricultural enterprise. The crops suffered; as a result, some farmers just picked up and left.

Pete Florsheim, heir to the Florsheim shoe family fortune, offers another glimpse into how developers squeezed out farmers in the 1950s. An environmentalist and lover of the great outdoors, Florsheim was uninterested in the family shoe business. He came to the Santa Clara Valley from Chicago in 1950 and bought acre upon acre of apricot orchards in South San Jose. On adjacent hillside land, he raised cattle. As juicy as the fruit that he grew in his orchards was his Western ranch style of entertaining: steer-neutering parties and barbecues, horseback riding and harvest festivals were common weekend pastimes at Pete's.

In time, though, home builders invaded the properties adjacent to his. Mischievous children moved in with their families; they raided Florsheim's orchards, disrupting the farming that he took so seriously. The cattle were agitated and so was Florsheim. He felt he had no choice but to sell and try to recreate the lifestyle he so cherished elsewhere. The Bay Area was changing rapidly from agricultural to industrial landscape, and open space was fast becoming a treasure of the past.

In the North County, open space at Stanford also was being consumed. Universities across the country were expanding to accommodate the many GIs who had come home in search of education, and Stanford was no different. Like other universities, Stanford needed an influx of funds to help pay for the GIs' education, house them, feed them, and expand university programs to accommodate greater numbers of students. But Stanford had one thing that many other universities did not: it had been endowed with 8,180 acres of so-called farmland.

Stanford also had an engineering dean with a keen interest in keeping the students he educated in the area. Once graduated and out of the university laboratories, Dean Frederick Terman's now famous engineer-entrepreneurs needed a place to pursue their enterprises. He did not want them to have to go east to be successful. At his urging, and in light of the need for funds to fuel the academic mission, Stanford's planning office converted a large chunk of its cattle range land into an industrial park to facilitate these young graduates' start-up businesses and to generate rental income.

The community favored the shift from cattle grazing to light industry concentrated around the research laboratories of a great university, and a large parcel of Stanford's acreage was set aside for such commercial use. Suddenly, Stanford's North County farmland had turned high tech. (Stanford's founding grant, conferring Leland Stanford's Palo Alto farm to the trustees of the university, stipulated that "these lands may never be sold." Thus, selling off parcels for income, luckily, was not an available income-generating option.)

Hewlett-Packard Company, founded in a Palo Alto garage by Stanford engineering students William Hewlett and David Packard, was an early occupant of the Stanford Industrial Park.

Sigurd and Russell Varian, who had worked directly under Dean Terman to develop the klystron tube, also were among the first to build in the industrial park. Their building was designed by Eric Mendelssohn, noted for designing the Einstein Tower in Israel and Maimonides Hospital in San Francisco.

Still another early tenant was Levinthal Electronics, founded by Elliott Levinthal, a former director of Varian Associates. Among his electronic devices were the defibrillator and the pacemaker, which are still in use for emergency heart therapy. Levinthal was no-nonsense: he favored good-quality construction for his utilitarian building, and he wanted ample parking for his employees. I was his architect, and I designed for mood and quality of life as well as quality of construction. I wanted to include landscaping as part of the design, to soften the parking lot and to screen the driveway. Such landscaping, however, took up space that could otherwise be used for parking. Demonstrating the difference between an engineer and an architect, we walked the grounds together, blueprints in hand, Levinthal crossing out the trees in the parking lots as fast as I could draw them, and both of us learning from each other. Levinthal was mentally calculating his annual income per employee, each of whom needed a parking spot. Fewer spots meant fewer employees, which meant less income. Multiplied over several years, Levinthal calculated that each parking spot was worth a substantial amount of money.

I blinked when I learned how much money he thought I would cost him with my trees.

The Stanford Industrial Park was also home to Watkins-Johnson, the West Coast offices of the *Wall Street Journal*, the research labs of Lockheed Missiles and Space Company, Xerox Corporation, and a host of other companies that would become pillars of Silicon Valley.

Farmland gave way not only to industrial development but also, eventually, to residential development. Similarly, my work for corporate clients also led to residential work—and to friendships. For example, I ultimately designed Levinthal's home on former farmland in Atherton, and together we built a spec house on the adjacent property. Unfortunately, I was relatively new to the area and not all that familiar with local flood plains. When a winter rainstorm flooded a creek near the property, the sold but still unoccupied spec house flooded, too, and Levinthal and I found ourselves bailing water from the basement in the middle of the night. We lost our sale, and most of the potential profit margin was eaten up recarpeting and repairing water damage, but the friendship survived.

While some companies leased the industrial park land from Stanford and built their own buildings, developers soon recognized a new opportunity to prosper. They began to lease the land from the university and put up buildings that they, in turn, would lease to companies. Jack Wheatley of Wheatley-Jacobson was one of these early developers. Following Stanford's carefully prescribed landscaping and parking requirements, Wheatley and other developers constructed quality buildings that met Stanford's strict design requirements.

Land use was changing. The shift from farmland to industrial and residential use now began, paving the way for future Silicon Valley businesses. Although the inexpensive open space had been an attractive element to a newcomer like me, the transformation from agricultural use to development was an essential step toward building Silicon Valley. But development would not be without its bumps: plenty of mistakes were made, and plenty of conflicts arose on the way to building a world-renowned technology center.

For example, Stanford's and Palo Alto's planners had not anticipated the extent of increased traffic to and from the industrial park, due largely to its growing workforce. By 1957, traffic had reached such a congested state all over Santa Clara County that major circulation problems ensued. Interstate 280 was added and the county developed its own expressway system. But even with these improvements, problems were rampant. Transportation remains a nagging problem in South Santa Clara County, and public transit issues continue to vie for government attention.

A local traffic problem illustrates the fine line that government officials must walk when addressing transportation issues.

In 1957, the City of Palo Alto proposed an initiative to convert the two-lane Oregon Avenue into a four-lane, two-way highway, with an underpass beneath the railroad tracks and Alma Street linking it to Page Mill Road. The proposed project would have cost 107 residents their homes. Ultimately, a compromise plan was reached that involved demolishing fewer homes. But even the compromise plan cost forward-thinking government leaders some friendships. Bud Hubbard was a Santa Clara County supervisor who could have bowed to the wishes of friends who lived on Oregon Avenue. Instead, he pursued what he thought was best for the long-term health of the community. Even with Oregon Expressway, there is still a very long six miles between east-west routes across the peninsula, spanning the distance from Woodside Road to Oregon Expressway.

Twenty years later, with Santa Clara County still struggling with traffic issues, Supervisor Rebecca Morgan advanced other solutions to growing circulation concerns. She played a major role in the long-awaited and long-delayed completion of Route 85, the cross-peninsula thoroughfare that connects u.s. 101 and Interstate 280 and eases the traffic load on each. Environmental groups in Saratoga who were opposed to a freeway passing by their secluded hamlet had held up the connector for years. The delay cost the taxpayers dearly both in traffic snags and in the price of the land needed to complete the traffic triangle. It was a major accomplishment to negotiate the land acquisition and construction.

The success of the Stanford Industrial Park not only required an examination of traffic routes but also demonstrated a new and effective way to make money in Santa Clara Valley. However, it was not necessarily a way that contributed to a healthy quality of life. Landowners, real estate developers, and speculators had already begun to demonstrate the tremendous opportunities that the San Francisco Peninsula offered. Many were making money hand over fist in speculative land and development deals. Profit taking had become the primary motivation of many of the businessmen in the area. And while construction in the Stanford Industrial Park was regulated by the university's planning office, development in the towns dotting the peninsula was not.

Stanford's planning office required proper setbacks from the street, quality construction, attractive landscaping, and excellent property management practices. In trying to recreate the industrial park in neighboring cities, including Palo Alto, Mountain View, Sunnyvale, and Santa Clara, developers were bound by none of the strict regulations that the university planning office imposed. Instead, they could buy small parcels zoned for light industrial use, erect large and inexpensive tilt-up buildings that often filled the properties edge-to-edge, and place the necessary heat, ventilation, and air-conditioning equipment on the roof to save space that could otherwise be rented. Many of the early developers thought that by maximizing rentable square footage and minimizing capital outlay, they would maximize the return on their investments. It would take years for them to learn that tenants not only were willing, but wanted to pay more per square foot for quality construction and appealing aesthetics.

This fearful approach—keeping investment at a minimum in the hope of maximizing return—was born of inexperience. In the early days of the valley, everyone was inexperienced. While these developers pursued profit by building on the cheap, city officials were not up to speed on such amenities as design, parking requirements, or adequate setbacks from the street. Only after the buildings went up and the streets became littered with cars that had nowhere else to park did the city officials begin to take notice and residents begin to complain. So did the building's tenants, who often had to walk blocks and blocks to work, only to arrive at unsightly buildings. With no attention or expenditure paid to architecture, landscaping, planning, or parking, these new buildings all too often were eyesores.

Within a year or two maintenance became a problem, too, as the air-conditioning and other mechanical equipment on the roofs began to rust. Buildings were left without heating or cooling systems for lengthy periods of time while owners scrambled to find repair companies. Roofs leaked. Water damage resulted. These were some of the prices paid for cutting corners.

Unlike the university planners, many of the upstart developers were not prepared to take on the role of property manager. They somehow assumed the properties would generate income without expenditures or attention to upkeep. But they learned quickly, particularly when their tenants vacated for higher-quality facilities, at higher rents. By voting with their feet, the tenants told the developers that there was more money to be made in doing things with an eye toward quality. Those with an intelligent approach to business responded and reaped the rewards.

In addition, land speculators were buying up larger properties and subdividing them for sale to real estate developers. If, as so often happened in the early days, the developer of the first lot erected a shoddy tilt-up rental building, the subsequent sales of the adjacent parcels were adversely affected. No one wanted to buy into a low-rent district. Soon enough, the speculators themselves were clamoring for regulations. Like the neighboring residents, they lobbied the local governments to require builders to use and develop good architecture, to put up buildings with important entrances and features, to landscape, and to provide sufficient parking for tenants.

City leaders heard the cries of foul from neighbors, speculators, and environmentalists and reacted strongly to the tilt-up boxes that now littered their outer rings and often abutted residential neighborhoods. In order to turn around the development of light industrial properties from shoddy, fast-buck operations to quality clean industry that was harmonious with the images the cities wanted to create for themselves, some cities hired consultants to help draft and impose design and building standards. Others began the arduous process of setting out zoning and building requirements. Some speculators, developers, and residents who would be directly affected by the evolving building regulations came forward to run for public office themselves, promising to clean up the light industrial zones in their towns.

What emerged from the morass, largely influenced by the Stanford planning office, was a caring, intelligent, and involved community that, once again, put a stake in the ground—this time, for quality real estate development. New regulations developed that limited the lot coverage of new buildings, based the number of required off-street parking spots on the square footage of building space, and imposed minimum setbacks from the street.

Aesthetics, in the form of landscaping, finishes, materials, and colors, also were regulated. The concept of a berm—a small hill abutting the sidewalk and landscaped to screen parked cars from the street—was developed and implemented in new industrial construction. The buildings were not ostentatious. They fit well with the California landscape.

Early Silicon Valley companies followed the model of the retail sector: they rented the space that they needed and spent their money on their businesses, not their buildings. But it soon became clear that in California, and particularly in Silicon Valley, the cost of land was appreciating so quickly that it made good financial sense to own. Rents inflated rapidly. As a result, many firms began to design and build their own facilities on their own property. These companies were growing, and they also needed adjacent reserve lands to protect themselves against highly inflated land costs in the future. This was not the case for the retail sector, which was not growing nearly as quickly as technology.

For the owner-occupants, many of whom made their bread and butter on government projects, there was a balance to be struck between form and function. They didn't want excessive, flashy buildings, but they didn't want shoddy construction, either. Architects engaged by government agencies and manufacturing firms that worked for the government had to strike the right balance for these new buildings: not so cheap that there were problems, but not so extravagant that they appeared exorbitant and expensive. They had to create a quality environment that demonstrated prudence in the way money was spent. Taxpayers and customers—then and now—logically deduce that they are footing the bill, through the taxes and fees that they pay, for agencies' or business firms' office space. They avoid doing business with firms that appear to have spent frivolously. So, in early Silicon Valley, where many projects were for county, state, or federal governments, a new goal was defined: that of a dignified office that reflected prudent but tasteful architecture and planning that was middle-of-the-road and not extreme.

The environment also posed a challenge to architects of these newer industrial parks. While the Stanford Industrial Park that they sought to emulate was nestled in the foothills, amid green, open space, the industrial density was much higher in the flatlands near the bay, and natural scenic beauty was lacking. It was very important to get good landscape architecture, thoughtful planning, and trees.

These commercial developers came to rely on real estate professionals to help lease their buildings. Agents and brokers saw it as their job to lease space, but they also felt an obligation to take care of the Silicon Valley entrepreneur. Soon, a network began to emerge among speculators, who made their profit by selling off land parcels; developers, who bought property and built on it for sale or rent; and real estate professionals, who matched the right tenants with the right landlords so that growth would be accommodated easily and all would prosper as a result. The real estate professionals worked with land speculators and project developers. They were the glue that held the network together, finding developers to buy from land speculators and tenants for the developers' projects. When a company outgrew its initial space, savvy real estate people worked with developers to help that company expand. Often, companies were willing to pay the developers partial rent while their new facilities were under construction. Real estate agents also helped the developers by finding new tenants to occupy spaces vacated by growing companies. Ideally, as a company expanded, adjacent office space would be available to them so that their existing operation could stay put while newer units were added in nearby offices. The development groups of Peery-Arrillaga, John Sobrato, and Carl Berg recognized this need for expansion and built entire industrial parks, moving businesses to bigger spaces within their parks as they grew.

Thus, high-tech companies found it easy to get office space, and, when they grew, they could expand at minimal moving costs.

Carl Berg provides an excellent example of how the real estate developer helped young companies to prosper. He had an eye for picking successful tenants, and he structured their leases to keep them as tenants. When, for example, entrepreneur Bob Fenwick wanted to rent space for a new venture in on-command video, now a standard amenity in hotel rooms across the country, Berg leased him a space that he could grow into. Fenwick needed only 10,000 square feet, he told Berg. Berg put him in a 25,000-square-foot space, charging him only for the portion he used and reserving the rest should Fenwick need more space down the line. When the company ultimately needed to expand, Berg released Fenwick from his original lease, signed him on for a larger portion of the space, and saved the young company the expense of moving while increasing his own rental income.

Berg would also sometimes modify his buildings to meet tenants' needs, accept company stock for rent, and occasionally invest in the tenant companies and serve on their boards of directors. He was a kinder, gentler venture capitalist, as Fenwick would explain years later, fair-minded, with modest demands and a fine reputation. But unlike contemporary venture capitalists, he did not require a formal business plan of the companies in which he invested; he relied on his instinct, and he wound up a Silicon Valley success himself.

Several other developers, including John Sobrato, John Arrillaga, Tom Ford, and Anthony P. "Tony" Meier also operated this way, with great success.

Developers and real estate professionals also worked with city governments to win approval for development of the various properties that they wanted to lease and/or sell. Without zoning, sewers, power lines, and roads, outlying parcels would not have been attractive investments. These interactions broadened the valley's expansion network to include civil engineers, soil engineers, public works officials, building and planning department officials, and fire marshals.

This real estate network worked for young high-tech companies in much the same way that a military outfit works for a new enlistee: basic needs were covered. Just as food, clothing, shelter, and a daily schedule of what to do and where to do it are provided to the new soldier, so space, utilities, and room to grow were provided to the start-up company in the early Silicon Valley.

Soon, land became so expensive that manufacturing was relocated to less pricey areas, such as Auburn, California, Austin, Texas, and the State of Oregon. This freed the former manufacturing sites to be redeveloped into more upscale, higher-rent office space.

At the most upscale end of the development spectrum, developer Tom Ford cast his eye on the green, rolling hills above Menlo Park, adjacent to Portola Valley and Woodside. Ford wanted to develop an office complex with as nice a look and feel as the Stanford Industrial Park. He worked with Menlo Park officials to win approval to develop acreage adjacent to Stanford abutting a new golf course, and he worked with architect Al Hoover on design concepts. Approval to build an office park in the open space of the foothills was a long shot. But the understated elegance of Hoover's proposed plans persuaded city officials that tasteful development could be a benefit to the region.

Today, Sand Hill Circle stands as a venture capital hub of one- and two-story buildings surrounded by beautifully maintained landscaping and catering to the crème de la crème. Its verdant hills and occasional benches are very much an extension of the university campus feel. A few minutes' drive from elegant homes in Atherton, Woodside, Portola Valley, and Los Altos Hills, Sand Hill Circle is a low-density, residential-style office park that has become the financial heart of Silicon Valley. Without the foresight of city officials, such a feather-in-the-cap complex would never have been possible. In this way, the role of city and county governments in the development of Silicon Valley was substantial: without their attention to planning, sensitivity to open space, and concern for overall quality of life, the region could not have become the success that it is today.

By the 1970s, the newly minted Silicon Valley was attracting cutting-edge technology businesses drawn to share in the energy and knowledge of already successful predecessors. But without a vibrant city life to sustain the people that came with these new ventures, the world-renowned companies might never have stayed. Cities had to improve the services and amenities they offered, or they risked losing the tax-base industries that seemed to be sprouting up as readily as prunes and apricots had a half-century earlier.

San Jose, in particular, was further challenged by City Manager Dutch Hamann's legacy. Inconsistent quality and an overabundant quantity of development in a strangely mapped city meant spotty city services in outlying areas and strained relations with neighboring cities.

This was the political landscape inherited in 1975 by San Jose's first woman mayor, Janet Gray Hayes. She was an environmentalist with a long family history of interest in the arts and a personal history of involvement in the community. She came into office with a strong sense that there was an opportunity to do better, especially in the area of planning. She favored cost-effective governance and provision of services. Her general bias was to slow the growth that City Manager Hamann had established as the San Jose way.

Hayes put the wheels in motion for the early stages of redevelopment, refocusing attention on the downtown area and hiring Frank Taylor as director of a new San Jose Redevelopment Agency. He, too, recognized that a vibrant downtown was an essential ingredient in recreating a habitable and hospitable city. Hayes set the tone for working cooperatively with other cities and rebuilding positive relationships with them. She allied herself with multiple organizations, ranging from Save the Bay to the Bay Conservation and Development Corporation.

Her tenure was not without tension. The old guard very much resented her major accomplishment: putting the brakes on growth in San Jose through tighter controls at the planning level. Although her policies hampered the ability of landowners and developers to make as much money as they had been making, slowing the rate of growth represented a major shift in San Jose toward quality of life.

A quite different mayor followed Janet Gray Hayes, but continued her forward momentum toward regentrification of a run-down city.

Tom McEnery had the advantage of being the first San Jose mayor elected under the strong mayor model, which he had worked as a council member to adopt. Up until his election in 1982, San Jose's mayor had no more authority than any other city council member did. As the first elected under

4

the new model, McEnery wielded far more power than his predecessors, and he used it.

McEnery was an affable Irishman, a great storyteller, and a longtime downtown resident. He was a colorful politician and a really sweet guy. And when it came to rebuilding his city, he minced no words and spared no effort. McEnery accomplished nothing short of rebuilding a city in desperate need of revitalization.

A national trend toward mega-malls had had a drastic effect on downtown San Jose. In the wake of the opening of the Valley Fair Shopping Center in San Jose in 1956, the downtown retail corridor had virtually emptied. With the arrival of Valley Fair, new large chain stores entered the valley, effectively destroying the smaller downtown merchants, who had far less buying power. Parking was free and easy at the mall; downtown still had street parking and meters. Weather was no deterrent to shopping at the mall, as it was fully enclosed, unlike downtown, where customers had to face the elements, whether rain or heat. The variety of items available in the mall far exceeded what the downtown merchants could provide. And the sparkling new feel of Valley Fair was a sharp contrast to the staid, old, dark buildings and grimy streets of downtown. Valley Fair was no mere competitor; it was a closer for local downtown stores and restaurants. Boarding up shops and closing stores led to another decline in the downtown neighborhood: with fewer resident merchants and passersby, a seedier element came to occupy the vacant store thresholds. Now prostitutes, winos, and bums inhabited the city center.

To revive the city center, McEnery enlisted local folks rather than big-name, nationally known experts in a homegrown sort of "promote from within" movement to engage the community in the work of rebuilding downtown. His goal? He wanted people to feel good about San Jose.

McEnery's administration aimed to rebuild the downtown. McEnery had a dream: to build the heart of Silicon Valley, a vibrant, people-centered city that would be busy with business ventures by day and enlivened by restaurants, clubs, theater, sports, and culture by night and on weekends. He envisioned a downtown park. He foresaw the best hockey arena in the nation. He dreamed of bustling hotels. His long-term plan was nothing short of electric.

The mayor used the city's redevelopment agency to prime the pump of development, starting with a 28.5 percent public investment in the new Fairmont Hotel. He made a decision to freeze tax revenues to the city at a certain level and to siphon off all tax revenue above that level to the redevelopment agency. He worked closely with Redevelopment Agency Director Taylor, an architect with a city-planning background who had more design sensitivity than most in his position. While many might view redevelopment on a project-by-project basis, Taylor looked beyond individual projects to create distinctive neighborhoods. His architectural background made for unusual solutions; his thoughtful, well-organized planning efforts ultimately replaced tattoo parlors, pool halls, and pawnshops with upscale boutiques, restaurants, and public buildings.

McEnery had the vision and Taylor had the know-how. Taylor shared then–council member McEnery's vision to revive the run-down city center. What's more, Taylor possessed the professional qualities necessary to make it happen. He brought McEnery's dream into focus and identified the steps that would have to be taken to make it reality.

Taylor brought a wide range of experience to the task. He had the capacity to help stimulate, create, and carry out the new mayor's goals. The challenge was daunting. A centerpiece convention center would attract visitors to San Jose, who would patronize restaurants, entertainment venues, and shopping opportunities during their free hours. But where would the conferees lodge? Taylor faced a chicken-and-egg dilemma: if the city built the convention center, but there were no fine hotels for the conventioneers to stay in, the convention center would sit vacant. If, on the other hand, hotels were built before the convention center, their rooms would sit empty and they would go out of business. Taylor had to figure a way to convince hoteliers to build in downtown San Jose at the same time that the convention center was going up, taking the gamble that conventions would draw paying guests. Amazingly, he was able to align the opening of the Fairmont and Hilton hotels in San Jose (encouraged by redevelopment agency money) with the opening of the new convention center.

With these two big pieces in place, the city was able to encourage the revival of restaurants in the downtown corridor, of museums, including The Tech Museum of Innovation and the Children's Discovery Museum, and the Performing Arts Center. Extending light rail from the outlying neighborhoods into the city center, repaving the streets, adding palm trees, and repairing sidewalks had a snowball effect, as higher-income local people now were attracted to downtown, too.

Soon, higher-income housing developed near the core of downtown. The once floundering City of San Jose was coming back to life. Together, McEnery and Taylor developed an overall master plan that transformed San Jose from an agricultural hub in the 1950s to the center of the high-tech world of the twenty-first century. They succeeded in attracting and retaining the business community, which provided the city not only with a strong tax base but also with a new moniker: The Capital of Silicon Valley.

The story of Town Park Towers, an early step in promoting housing and healthy development in the core of the city, offers an interesting look at how the work of cleaning up downtown was accomplished.

The First Presbyterian Church of San Jose hired me to provide drawings for construction of a new roof for their chapel. I went down to take a look at the building and, my God! was it dilapidated! The smell of mildew assaulted me when I walked in the front door. The leaking roof had created numerous problems. And while the roof definitely needed replacement, the building had been neglected for so long that it would have been impossible to get approval for the new roof from the building department, which was concerned with the overall condition of the building. A new roof for this building would have required an engineer's signature. But no engineer could make calculations with figures from 1890 construction drawings, and the scrutiny of a structural engineer would have required undue and costly testing. There was no budget for engineering, let alone engineering tests, nor was there any way of raising the money to pay for this expensive procedure.

I was a young architect, and I badly needed the work. I am also a human being; I hadn't the heart to walk away from these kind folks, no matter how problematic their project was.

I could see that the plan they had proposed could not be accomplished. The neighborhood, adjacent to downtown, had evolved considerably. When it was built in the late 1800s, wealthy families inhabited its grand, Eastern-style homes with broad front porches and windowed attic lofts. These same families had built and supported the neighborhood churches. But when the upscale population moved out to the suburbs, as was the case in so many American cities, they built new churches for themselves near their new homes, leaving the old church buildings to the lower-income families who moved in and couldn't afford to support them. Now a third migration had taken place. The rambling old homes of the turn-of-the-century had been converted into rooming houses. Their majestic porches were sagging; their cedar shingles thirsted for paint. And more than one had been boarded up due to fire caused by an elderly boarder cooking on a hot plate in his room. Just as Mayor McEnery wanted to bring the city back to life, so I wanted to help these folks with their church, which was so important to the health of this neighborhood. I had to think, and I had to work with the congregation to come up with a workable idea.

What could we do for the future of this neighborhood? How could we make a greater statement than a roof on a church? Could we possibly consider housing and other social conditions as we considered our next steps?

After weeks of pondering this predicament, I finally came up with a possible but ambitious solution: to take down the existing church, which was suffering from so many structural problems, subdivide the acreage it stood on, build a senior housing project on one parcel, and erect a smaller version of the church building on the other. At that time, the federal office of Housing and Urban Development was offering grant money for senior housing projects, and I thought that this group could qualify. If we could get the government support, and were very, very careful with budget allocations and expenditures, there might be enough money to build both the housing project and the church, which, presumably, could serve some of the project's senior residents.

A great solution by a brilliant young architect, right?

Wrong.

When I presented the idea to the congregation, the mere notion of taking down their building provoked outrage and tears.

"My mother contributed that chandelier," one congregant said sadly.

"What about all the memorial plaques on the pews?" another wondered. "How will those people be remembered in a new building?"

"My grandfather's name is on one of the pews," someone added in a whisper.

Town Park Towers, circa 1970

Town Park Towers began as a roof replacement project and ended up as a senior housing complex and adjacent Presbyterian church.

Emotions ran high as we discussed razing the existing, dilapidated church and erecting a new one with the help of Housing and Urban Development funds, which would require us to build senior housing as well.

Salvaging certain sentimental touches, including a stained-glass window and the old church bell, resulted in an urban development project in which the community could take great pride.

"The stained-glass windows were designed by my grandfather," said another.

And so it went.

Leveling a community's spiritual home was not as easy as razing a barn.

"What if we could salvage those pews?" I wondered aloud.

Maybe we could reuse the light fixture, I thought. What would it take to disassemble a stained-glass window, store it, and reinstall it in a new church building? I wondered.

As I listened to my client-congregants, I learned. Unlike corporate or government buildings, a church chisels sacred space out of the ordinary. It collects and retains the life of its community as the significant events of individual lives take place within its walls. Baptisms, first communions, confirmations, weddings, funerals—these are meaningful milestones that we cling to and treasure. They cannot, and should not, be wiped away. Nor should the structural marker that jogs the memory of them fall victim to a building code.

Together, my firm and the congregation figured a way to make the plan work.

Then came the work of applying to the government for funding, which required meeting all sorts of government requirements that were new to me. I had worked with local governments, but the challenge of the federal government was something else again.

In the end, it was a story of success. A fully occupied 212-unit senior housing project sits on the property now. We built a beautiful little church adjacent to it, reusing many of the sentimental finishes and furnishings from the original building, including its bell tower, which serves as a piece of sculpture at the entrance to the new church building.

At the grand opening of the new facilities, an elderly resident of the apartment building approached me and asked if I'd like a tour of the building. I accepted with pleasure. She showed me through the church, pointing out the special details and touches that remained from the original building, then took me through the apartment house, finally arriving at her room.

"Would you like to see the inside?" she asked.

As we sat in her room, she began to tell me her life story—her upbringing, her married life, and how naively she had carried on, allowing her parents and her husband to make her way for her. After her husband passed away, she knew nothing about how to fend for herself, she told me. Distraught and without resources, this once comfortable woman had ended up on the streets.

"But now look," she beamed. "Here I am in my own apartment. I am so lucky, so grateful. Did you ever see anything like it?"

I admitted to her then that I was the architect who had designed this, her new home.

The neighborhood today is consistent with McEnery's vision. It is vibrant and mixed, with many Vietnamese shops and markets. It is gratifying to see a lively, family-oriented community centered around a church that not so long ago stood wobbly, awaiting the wreckers' ball.

In addition to the Town Park Towers project, cheap rooming houses had to be replaced with middle-class housing, apartment complexes for seniors, and office buildings that would bring people into the city to support the new businesses there. Combining redevelopment agency money with developers' money made it possible to build quality apartments, to bring in light rail, and to install granite sidewalks planted with trees and surrounded by fountains and public art. A major convention center, the best hockey arena in the country, an upscale centerpiece hotel, and refurbished older hotels make San Jose's center, once inhabited by undesirables, a lively nightspot.

Finally, McEnery's leadership in the Guadalupe River Park project turned a waterway polluted with industrial waste into a downtown park complete with a children's museum and pedestrian malls where people can stroll or eat their lunch. A relatively healthy river in the 1900s, by the 1980s the Guadalupe had become a place to dump industrial waste. McEnery and other civic leaders worked with officials from the state Department of Fish and Wildlife and with environmentalists to return the river to its natural state and to reutilize it as a necessary part of the flood control system. Walkways were set back from the river so as not to disturb the wildlife now inhabiting the water's edge. The Guadalupe River Park project is yet another example of how McEnery inspired the community to rehabilitate the city, clean up the river, and build an enviable quality of life in a city once plagued by urban blight.

Other California cities also tried to redevelop their downtowns with pedestrian malls to encourage leisurely shopping. These efforts were largely unsuccessful, because only stores on the outer perimeter that were visible from the street could entice people to park their cars and come in to shop. Storefronts inside courtyards were far less compelling; they did not have street frontage and were therefore shopped only by people who knew about them and sought them out especially. The lack of visibility made these stores secondary locations, and they suffered. Soon, such malls were half-empty as store after store without street-front space went out of business.

More successful were smaller cities' attempts to increase foot traffic with public celebrations. Annual art and wine festivals and ethnic festivities, such as Cinco de Mayo celebrations, Chinese New Year parades, Christmas and Hanukkah activities, merchant-sponsored trick-or-treating at Halloween, and children's sporting competitions brought a mix of people downtown who often stayed, or later returned, to eat and shop. In Palo Alto, where snow is unheard of, the downtown merchants combined efforts for years to hold a Snowballs and Sleigh Rides event every December, importing and dumping tons of snow into the main downtown artery for an evening winter festival that included horse-drawn sleigh rides and the once-a-year opportunity to build snowmen and engage in snowball fights in a town where it never snows.

Not to be outdone by folksier, smaller neighbors, San Jose parks also picked up on the nostalgia kick. A large downtown park features a petting zoo, a kiddie railroad, picnic areas, and sporting fields; another park is home to a bandstand, fountains, and outdoor art. The redevelopment agency generally and Frank Taylor specifically are most often credited with the infusion of activity and energy in San Jose. Taylor successfully transformed San Jose into a city that stands independent of San Francisco, its more famous neighbor to the north, offering outstanding cultural activities, nightlife, shopping, and dining.

Taylor did not have to build San Jose from scratch. One thing Silicon Valley had on its side was infrastructure. When Taylor took the helm of the redevelopment agency, there existed a plethora of industry, some dating back as far as 1912, that meant he did not have to worry about where building materials would come from, where to find quality construction crews, or how to communicate with the foreman on a job site. As early as 1909, Stanford University President David Starr Jordan had provided "venture capital" to a recent graduate named Cyril Elwell, who launched a wireless communications company called Federal Telegraph Company. It quickly grew into the area's largest electronics business and achieved significant advances in the development of radio.

Electronics companies, radio and microwave labs, engineering firms, aerospace industry, wiring, and carpentry and craft shops already were established in the region, largely as an outgrowth of research done at Stanford. Federal contracts, university lab support, the Cold War, and the space race ensured the success of firms like Fairchild Semiconductor, IBM, General Electric Computers and General Electric Microwave, Hewlett-Packard, Lockheed Aircraft, and Philco. Over time, many creative and forward-thinking individuals who were already part of the technological workforce shifted their focus to the development of innovative electronics and even entire industries. Ingenious inventions came out of their work, such as audio- and videotape, integrated circuits, lasers, random access storage, memory chips, microprocessors, computerized telephone systems, and thousands of other innovations that have changed our world. To this day, cross-fertilization of related ideas and integration of unrelated industries keep Silicon Valley a synergistic hub of innovation and creativity. Already by the 1950s, data storage technologies, transistors, and integrated circuits were as much a part of the landscape as apricots had been a decade earlier.

Infrastructure made the birth of Silicon Valley possible, and infrastructure sustains the enterprise. Just as the most famous American dress designers have based their businesses in New York City, where they have immediate access to the tools of their trade, so those engaged in emerging technologies gravitate toward Northern California, where the marketplace of ideas and existing infrastructure fuel their creative efforts. In New York, designers have immediate access to fabric markets, workrooms, models, photographers, and media. A talented individual who set up shop in a small Midwestern town would be isolated and far less likely to succeed than in New York. Similarly, those interested in high technology migrate to Silicon Valley, where opportunities abound and access to research centers such as Xerox's Palo Alto Research Center and an international brain trust at Stanford augment the region's burgeoning computer hardware, software, networking, and Internet businesses.

What else did new entrepreneurs need in the way of infrastructure?

They needed housing, schools, and stores, and industrious nontechnical newcomers improved the quality of all of these amenities.

As I mentioned, the upscale shopping mall had replaced the old-style downtown district and the revamped downtown had not yet emerged. A local conflict between challenge and opportunity illustrates the impact of growth on a community.

While the Palo Alto community generally had supported the Stanford Industrial Park, the university's next land development venture was largely met with trepidation by merchants and local property owners. The proposed Stanford Shopping Center created more friction between Palo Alto and Stanford than anything that has come up since. Although Stanford officials claimed that the shopping center would strengthen a "buy on the Peninsula" mentality, the decision to bring large San Francisco retailers to the Peninsula virtually shut down downtown Palo Alto, at least for a time. Palo Alto's small downtown district, like those in Menlo Park and Los Altos, included men's and women's clothing stores, specialty shops, and a few restaurants, but no department stores. University Avenue's lack of off-street parking and the Stanford Shopping Center's abundance of it led customers to flock to the new retail center, which opened in 1956 with 45 stores. Many downtown merchants followed their clientele to the Stanford Shopping Center, leaving many University Avenue storefronts vacant. Others, like Gleim Jewelers, ultimately operated a downtown location and a store at the shopping center. More than a few businesses went bankrupt while agonizing over whether to beat 'em or join 'em, as downtown turned into ghost town and the shopping center grew up around anchor stores including I. Magnin, Joseph Magnin, the Emporium, and later Macy's and Bullock's.

Angered though the Chamber of Commerce was over the retail center, the fact was that the community needed a regional shopping center. The population had grown large enough to sustain a major retail center. Busy lives and lifestyles were emerging on the Peninsula, with school activities, children's theater, and after-school sports clubs, not to mention the new hospital and many arts and charitable organizations. Many people were finding so much to do in their own emerging community that they had limited time to travel to San Francisco for access to big department stores.

Today, Palo Alto is far better off than it would have been without the Stanford Shopping Center. The hefty taxes that the center generates for the city of Palo Alto have fortified city finances and programs, allowing the development of such amenities as a children's theater program, a children's museum and zoo, a community aquatic center, and extensive cultural and recreation activities and classes, which are offered and subsidized by the city. Having found new avenues for success and remedied earlier drawbacks, such as a lack of off-street parking, by building lots and garages, the downtown district today is flourishing. A dense, close-in housing core offers residents the opportunity to walk to town to drink coffee, shop, dine, or people-watch. Responding to the shopping center with new, unusual, and upscale specialty stores, restaurants, and nightlife, downtown Palo Alto has become a fashionable Northern California destination spot.

But in the 1950s, this eventual peaceful coexistence was not so obvious, and the mall's upscale retailers left a void in the middle-income retail market. During this time of explosive development, many in the Santa Clara Valley made their living in construction and the trades that supported building projects. For them, there seemed to be a gap between the fashionable department stores and the clothes and housewares that they thought suited them.

Enter Mervin Morris, hailing from Delano, California, who married and settled in the Bay Area in 1949. Morris envisioned a department store to serve the area's middle class. Mervyn's positioned itself in between the major department stores, such as Macy's, Bullocks, and The Emporium, which carried name-brand merchandise, and stores like Sears and J. C. Penney, which offered goods manufactured under in-house labels, such as Kenmore and Craftsman.

Mervyn's was just becoming established in the mid-1950s, about the same time that suburban flight and shopping malls were killing downtown marketplaces. Morris deduced that his stores must be located in the suburbs, where the people were, not in the city centers, from which people were fleeing. The trick was to locate in areas adjacent to housing tracts inhabited by the kind of customer that the Mervyn's stores served: quality-conscious, middle-income people who wanted to wear name brands but did not want to pay Macy's prices. The first Mervyn's store was built in San Lorenzo in a freestanding building unattached to a shopping mall. Its departments included housewares, bed and bath, jewelry, and shoes and clothing for the entire family, all at reasonable prices.

Just as real estate brokers would later play a major role in facilitating the growth of high-tech start-ups by identifying and expanding space for their clients, so a real estate broker was instrumental in the rise of the Mervyn's chain. After the first store opened, a broker approached Morris, explaining that a Fremont property was being developed into a shopping center and the developer needed an anchor tenant. Morris was looking to expand, and the new shopping center seemed to provide an ideal opportunity.

Over the years, Morris recognized the value that a capable real estate broker could provide, and he engaged Linn Miller to help him identify and develop new sites for Mervyn's stores. New suburbs were springing up all over the Bay Area, and many retailers gambled, building stores where they anticipated that new roads and developments would someday be built. Morris never took that chance. The gamble that some of his competitors engaged in, building at the intersections of yet unconstructed arteries, could mean a big payoff. But building on inexpensive land in the middle of nowhere with the hope that it soon would become a population hub could also mean financial ruin. If the planned roadways were delayed, rerouted, or never built, the shopping centers built in anticipation of them remained in the middle of nowhere. So the job of the real estate broker was not only to identify good land and strike a good deal, but also to possess the vision to see what the future would look like in the growing valley. The broker's network necessarily included urban planners and developers. These contacts would be invaluable in the coming years, as the Santa Clara Valley blossomed into Silicon Valley and real estate professionals became an integral link in leasing and development cycles. But for Morris, the costs associated with building and then waiting for the population to follow were too high. He never opened a store where housing was not yet established.

Morris prospered. When he first went into business, he thought that if he could make $1 million, he would be the happiest guy in the world. Suffice it to say that when he sold the Mervyn's chain to the Dayton Hudson Company in the 1990s, he retired a very, very, very happy man.

While the real estate community was gearing up to meet the opportunity that the high-technology revolution would bring, businessman Stuart Moldaw saw yet another retail opportunity. He bought designer close-outs and discounted them in his newly launched Ross Stores. In time, he would find that the best deals were those based on American designs but manufactured overseas, where the labor costs were much lower.

This discovery was a foreshadowing of the electronics industry of today, where American ingenuity is responsible for design and manufacturing is procured abroad. As the valley transitioned from low-cost agricultural land to high-priced, developed office parks and custom homes, Silicon Valley firms began moving their manufacturing plants out, initially to domestic sites such as Austin, Phoenix, Central California, and Oregon and, later, overseas to Hong Kong, Taiwan, China, Indonesia, and Malaysia, as well as to Mexico. Engineering, design, and administration were retained in Silicon Valley, largely because the corporate executives did not want to leave. The resulting housing expansion would produce a distinctive California style of architecture that ultimately shaped a way of life and new ways of working in Silicon Valley.

Northern California architecture has a look and feel all its own, a look and feel that was inspired by the mild climate and scenic beauty of the Bay Area and developed into a way of living, thinking, and working creatively. As young technology companies prospered, their executives began to engage architects to design homes for them that capitalized on Northern California's considerable amenities. In time, the lifestyles that these business leaders came to enjoy influenced the style and tone of tract home development and also reshaped the business leaders' thoughts about the workplace, leading the most visionary of them to transform the business environment from factory into corporate campus.

East Coast buildings are boxy by necessity. Keeping out the very cold air that can dip into the single digits in winter and insulating against the very hot and humid weather that can rise to triple digits in summer demands fewer exterior walls and smaller windows to minimize exposure to unfriendly elements. In the East, an architect's primary concerns are a good floor plan within the box shape and respect for existing neighborhoods.

Such was not the case for post–World War II architects building in temperate Northern California. Full-acre properties with year-round foliage provided privacy, making consistency with a neighboring house's style a less important concern. Landscaping fills in quickly in Northern California and stays full all twelve months of the year, so design does not have to account for bare twigs in winter, which make houses the only points of interest on a horizon. Less insulation is needed; glass treatments can be larger and more creative; storm windows are unnecessary; and heating and cooling loads are much more manageable. In an area blessed with mild climate and an abundance of breathtaking vistas, architects found a new freedom in designing both residential and commercial buildings that would take best advantage of the particular property and its views. They could create gardens as outdoor living rooms and offer flexible year-round uses of both indoor and outdoor space.

The region's long history of architecture that works with nature now manifested itself in custom homes built for executives of the emerging technology industries. Uninspired by the cavelike buildings of their Midwestern and East Coast childhoods, these clients wanted to make use of their whole properties, not only viewing outdoor gardens and vistas, but flowing seamlessly from indoors to outdoors and back in again. This was accomplished in a number of different ways. Slate or granite floors could run from a living room out to a patio, creating the illusion that the outdoors was an extension of the indoor living space. Bedrooms projecting from the central block of

5

the house were possible in Northern California's warmer climate, where bedrooms did not have to be framed by four interior walls to stay warm. With three exterior, windowed walls, much more natural light streamed into the room, and views—whether of garden or mountain or valley—could be enjoyed from the comfort of a home's most intimate spaces. No longer as limited by heavy heating and cooling demands, raised ceilings, some with skylights, offered a feeling of spaciousness and elegance. Eastern-style decks and balconies, which enhanced the three-dimensional interest of a home's exterior but were not wide enough for outdoor use, were adapted to become expansive decks, broad enough for dining, recreation, and relaxation out-of-doors. Free of the concern about snow loads, these balconies grew from three- to five-foot widths to ten- to twenty-foot widths and more, with slatted railings that allowed views of the gardens from the interior of the house as well as from the deck.

I brought these concepts to the spec house that I built on a ridge in the Los Altos Hills in 1952, when I first came to California. Perhaps the design was before its time, or perhaps the house, just a little further out than the next closest development, was considered by buyers to be too far from town. In any case, it was not a quick sale, and I spent weekend after weekend showing brokers and potential buyers through the house, which I had built as an example of my California design work.

The California house in the hills brought back memories of Glencoe, Illinois. Back in Glencoe, I had won a *Better Homes and Gardens* magazine's five-star plan for a house that I had built for myself. I trotted the magazine around everywhere, to show off to potential clients, realtors, and homebuyers. What I didn't necessarily tell them was the lesson I had learned from building and selling the showplace house, which had won such a prestigious award.

When I graduated from college I had built a charming, two-story home on a friendly, residential street in Evanston, Illinois. One block from a hospital, a block and a half from a bus stop, and a short distance from schools and shopping, the house sold quickly and easily when we decided to build a bigger house on a larger lot in Glencoe.

Though the Glencoe property was further out and much more rural than the neighborhood we had left, we were able to buy an acre of land on a golf course that was just developing. I designed an elegant, one-story home, the one *Better Homes and Gardens* selected as one of its five-star plans. We lived there and loved it for two years, but when we decided to move to California, it was time to sell. Even though the award-winning home was well-designed and very attractive, there wasn't near the volume of interest that we enjoyed when we sold our Evanston home. The mantra of the real estate industry is location, location, location. Though Glencoe would grow to become an affluent and desirable Chicago suburb, it was not there yet. Our house was one of the first to be built in an area that was just being developed. Our buyer knew that the Glencoe location did not appeal to the many buyers who sought closer-in properties. Our buyer knew that we were anxious to leave; we already had said our good-byes to family and friends, who were pressuring us to reconsider and stay. But as the close-of-sale date approached, the buyer began a series of delaying tactics. For example, he called our attorney to complain that a water main had been discovered under the property. He demanded more time to review the situation.

Weeks went by. Our attorney advised us that the pipe was an excuse: the buyer's real goal was to reduce the sale price. He suggested that we set a date for closing the sale, and that after that date, if the deal was not done, the house would go back on the market. We were hesitant to draw the line. We had had only one offer in four weeks, and the price was the lowest that we could accept. If this deal fell through, who knows how long it would be before another buyer came along?

A week and a half later we reached a decision. I called the buyer directly and told him, "We close by 2 P.M. tomorrow or the house goes back up for sale."

At 2 o'clock the next day the sale was closed.

From this experience came two more life lessons: timing can be everything, and sometimes you have to draw the hard line in order to get where you are going.

The California house in the hills brought back memories of Glencoe. The California house was intended as a marketing piece to showcase my ability, just as the Glencoe house had attracted *Better Homes and Gardens'* attention. The house sat on six acres, with majestic vistas offering a 280-degree view overlooking both the valley toward the bay and a range of hills projecting one over the other. But surprise costs, including bringing the utilities a quarter mile up the hill, and a thin budget meant that I had run out of money before paving the driveway. If visitors got a good running start up the gravel, they had no problem. But those who took it slow often spun out. This, plus the distance from town, made the property hard to sell.

So when the one-year lease on my rented house in the flatlands ran out and still the house on the hill sat empty, I decided to move in myself. Meanwhile, some of those who had seen the house had liked it enough to ask me to design custom homes for them on their own lots. While I was quite successful in designing their houses, I was far less successful in selling mine. But fate can unwittingly play a role in changing people's perceptions. Suddenly, I found myself very busy with clients and projects, and instead of being seen as a struggling architect, I was perceived as "that successful young architect who lives in the big, beautiful house in the hills."

In those early days, many developers—even custom home developers—worked without architects, using draftsmen to offer a client four or five standard designs. By allowing clients to make minor adjustments, these developers gave their clients a custom impression with a set of rehashed plans. Little or no attention was paid to a specific property's location, orientation, contour, or other characteristics. They did not take into account the views, the breezes off the bay, or the existing landscape, often destroying old native oaks in the foothills. They altered the site to fit the blueprint, not the other way around.

To me, choosing the right site and situating a building on it to take advantage of all its benefits is the most important aspect of architecture. Creating a site plan for each individual lot and developing a floor plan with attention to the grades of the terrain and views from each room of mountains and bay establishes the necessary foundation for a beautiful piece of architecture that supports the lifestyle of its residents. A competing architect's inattention to this sensitive balance brought me one of my early California clients.

Appalled by a developer's proposal to lop off the top of her newly purchased Portola Valley hill property and place a stock house on top of it, professional dancer and environmentalist Adelaide Hutton returned to her real estate broker and demanded her money back, including his commission. She said that the site was unsuitable for building the environmentally sensitive home she wanted.

The broker had shown many clients through my house and had heard me talk about fitting a design to a site, "working" a house to fit the slopes between existing trees, and taking advantage of hilltop views. He asked Mrs. Hutton to talk to me before she made a final decision to void the sale.

The other architect had tried to reshape the Huttons' hill to accommodate the house design that he already had on paper, shaving off the top of the site, including all the trees. Instead, we talked about how to shape the building to fit the hill, dropping one room lower and raising another room higher to fit the grade. We wanted to use sensitivity and skill, working a house between existing natural landscaping like a piece of lace cut in, among, and around the trees. Glass treatments would allow varying views from many angles in each room. The house was to be built on thirty-inch posts tied together with a concrete frame of grade beams that would be hidden by raised, floating floors. This pier system would allow us to create a comfortable living area that harmonized with nature. It would protect the existing mature trees' root systems and take full advantage of the trees' beauty as they peeked and poked through decks surrounding the house to create a very natural environment. The house itself was to be a series of glass gazebos, allowing its residents truly to live in nature. Largely based on the vision we discussed, the Huttons became convinced to let us develop the property.

In the Hutton house, we used multilevel floor planes both inside and out to accommodate the hill and allowed existing trees to poke up through the redwood decks outside. The pool was consciously placed and oriented toward the mountains to avoid the cool breezes that blow off the bay in the summer. A stone fireplace, wide expanses of glass, and high ceilings were incorporated into the house. Exposed indoor beams and glass exterior walls created an indoor-to-outdoor transition that felt seamless and allowed for views to mountains and trees from all directions. Teaming up with Geraldine Knight Scott, a landscape architecture professor from the University of California at Berkeley, ensured that the landscaping was part of the living space, whether it was occupied, as it was in the summer months, or viewed from inside, as it was during the winter months. Paint colors were selected to match the tree bark. Awareness of the microclimate for outdoor living

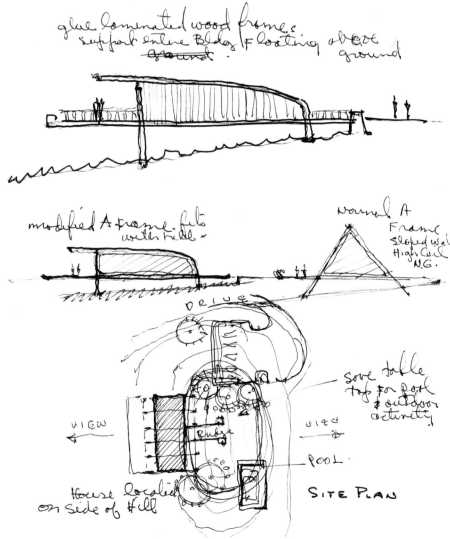

Residential projects were a mainstay of our practice from the time that we arrived in California in 1952. Among the most distinctive for their seamless indoor-to-outdoor living spaces are the homes in the following pages.

Dawson residence, circa 1955

Before he became a United States Senator, Alan Cranston worked in real estate. Through him, I met Mr. and Mrs. Larry Dawson, who owned thirty acres of land in Los Altos Hills. They wanted a creative home to fit on a magnificent ridge that had unobstructed views to the bay on one side and the mountains on the other.

comfort, attention to the contours of the property and its foliage, and respect for the natural beauty of the site resulted in an innovative and delicate home that was sensitive to the surrounding foothills. The building simply grew with the shrubbery and trees right out of the land.

When architects partner with landscape designers and craftsmen, the overall end-product can be environmentally sensitive, aesthetically pleasing, and very livable. It was not long before developers of the less expensive tract housing that was needed to accommodate a rapidly growing California employee base followed the lead of architects designing custom homes. Though the houses were necessarily smaller and less detailed, they emulated the flavor of California design, with windows, skylights, open floor plans, and developed outdoor spaces. These homes helped to develop the special quality of life prevalent throughout the San Francisco Bay Area for people at all income levels.

Government plays an important role in the building process, steering and balancing the need for development with quality of development. Ideally, government guidelines ensure proper setbacks, tree-lined streets, and sensitivity to the environment while allowing reasonable construction at reasonable costs so that a community can change and grow in a balanced way.

But sometimes the public will question regulation. An interesting rebellion took place in Palo Alto when the residents perceived the government as going too far in one direction. In trying to protect existing homes, the city inadvertently imposed an inflexible ordinance that failed to recognize the difference between historic homes and houses that were simply old. The city also did not heed the shift from a graying population of homeowners to younger, more affluent residents with families.

In the 1990s, Palo Alto instituted special interim guidelines with regard to remodeling historic buildings, including private homes. "Historic" was defined as structures built before 1940. This was consistent with the secretary of the interior's historic standard, which applied to buildings fifty years old or older. In Palo Alto, in addition to a Historic Resources Board that had to approve building plans before they could be submitted to the building department for permit, the city contracted with a preservation architect, who reviewed homeowners' remodeling plans before the Historic Resources Board did. She had all but veto power over plans she did not like. To add insult to injury, only half her fees were charged to the city; the homeowners applying for her approval were charged for the other half—whether or not they ultimately won her support—when they submitted their plans to the city for review.

Trying to upgrade older homes into livable family spaces while retaining a modicum of historic integrity was a noble plan. But the interim process was so unpredictable, so arduous, and so cumbersome that city voters ultimately threw out the preservation architect and the interim ordinance, and, when the city council came up with a seemingly reasonable compromise plan, the angry electorate voted it down in referendum. The voters were in

I learned early through *Sunset Magazine* and fellow architects that a team approach to design was desirable in California. With its mountains, valleys, and uniquely landscaped terrain, the landscape architect played a stronger role than in the Midwest, where I came from. While the architect focused on the building, the landscape architect focused exclusively on how the building worked with the site, resulting in much stronger solutions. I was fortunate early in my career to meet Thomas Church, a respected leader in his field, and have been lucky enough to have had the opportunity to work with him for more than thirty years on fifteen different homes. The Dawsons' was the first.

The art of placing houses on hills has many options. A house can straddle the hill with building elements on both sides; it can cut through the hill; it can cut into the hill on one side or both sides; it can follow the ridge of the hill; it can be part on top, part on the side; or it can step down the hill with multiple stories. I mention these options because working with Thomas Church was the education that helped me really understand the complexity of this art form.

On this particular house, we used a modified A-frame. The entire house shifted to the side of the hill, leaving the top for parking, a swimming pool, and other outdoor activities. We manufactured flat land by making the floor of the house tangent with the top of the hill. We used laminated wood members, floating decks, and the modified A-frame to achieve this look.

Pritzker residence, circa 1960

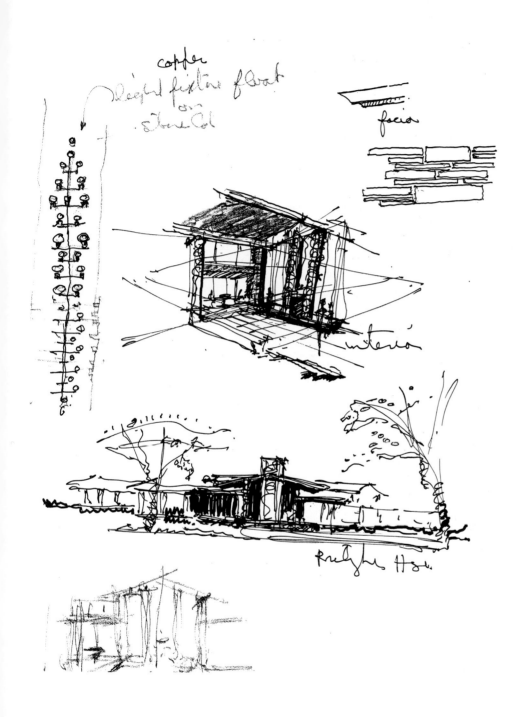

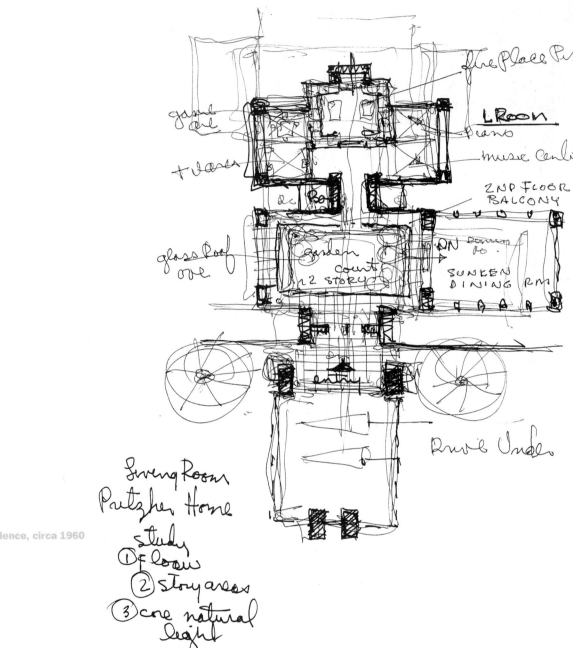

Pritzker residence, circa 1960

no mood to compromise, and the pendulum swung a little too far in the other direction. That's our system.

This is an example of government overstepping its intended function by imposing regulations that seem unreasonably strict. Some people felt this was the case statewide when then-Governor Jerry Brown prescribed a state energy ordinance that required certain levels of insulation for walls, glass, and ceilings, and limited the size of openings to the exterior of a building. The result restricted residents' design choices and imposed unnecessary costs. The cost of this energy ordinance has been extraordinary: whole new government departments have developed to enforce it, not only at the state level, where the rules were enacted, but also at the local level, where they are enforced. Lawyers, engineers, administrators, plan checkers, building inspectors, and more are employed to oversee the implementation of the energy ordinance on every building in California. Architects hire consultants at the owners' expense to meet the requirements of the regulation. Architects have argued that the economics of energy lead to self-regulation, and that the higher utility bills that result from poorly insulated structures lead occupants to choose a proper level of insulation. They have argued that some clients prefer to have a larger window, and wear a sweater, than to have smaller openings imposed on them. We have pointed out that the major utility companies operating in the state offer incentive programs for energy conservation measures, and these, too, lead to conservative use of resources. But the arguments have fallen on deaf ears, and the energy ordinance remains in place. With many people now making their livelihood enforcing this measure, it is unlikely to be dismantled any time soon, if ever.

Silicon Valley was growing much more rapidly than the rest of the nation. The meteoric expansion of housing, retail, commercial, and industrial development forced local governments to expand to meet the communities' changing needs. Courts processed more cases, hospitals treated more patients, transit systems carried more passengers, roads carried more cars. As cities in Silicon Valley grew, they began to build staffs to manage their more complex problems. More meetings, more people to manage the complexity, and more elected boards, too, evolved as checks and balances for moderate and appropriate growth.

During this period of rapid growth and change, construction improvements on residential housing tracts were achieved incrementally, making small, step-by-step improvements. Often, builders would make a minor adjustment in a competitors' design to end up with a look or feature that set them apart—a process that was a far cry from the creative innovation taking place in Silicon Valley by 1975.

Irwin Mittelman and Bob Reese were good friends of mine. I had had the opportunity to design "Mitt"'s Atherton home and he loved it—so much so that he asked me to help design a new tract of two-story homes in the rapidly developing city of Cupertino in the early 1960s. Mittelman and Reese bought acreage to accommodate one hundred houses, and we designed three floor

Steinberg residence, circa 1970

Oshman residence, circa 1981

Oshman residence, circa 1981

Crosby residence, circa 1976

Fenwick residence, circa 1985

Bob Fenwick and his wife, Jan, are both products of Stanford University. Bob is one of many success stories in high-tech electronics. After selling Bob's first major company, the Fenwicks asked me to look at forty acres in Los Altos Hills, where they wanted to build a new home. Influenced by the small Eichler they had lived in, they wanted something creative, original, aesthetic, and fun. The house was designed to take advantage of 360-degree views.

Over the years, the Fenwicks have opened their home to the public for political, charitable, and environmental benefits.

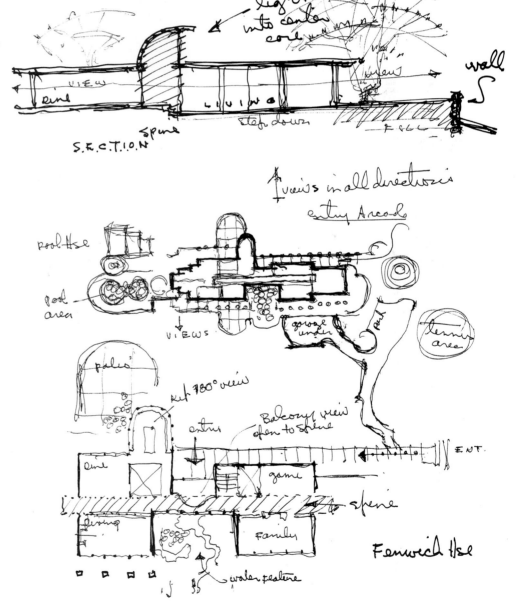

House residence, circa 1995

House residence, circa 1995

plans, each with three different exterior elevations, yielding nine houses that each looked different. By making the same plans left-handed and right-handed and changing color schemes, we were able to make every house in the subdivision look individualized.

Incorporating architectural design features and developing the project with architectural planning separated Mittelman and Reese's homes from the draftsmen's plans their competitors used. Their 1,800-square-foot house was competing against another very successful developer's 2,000-square-foot house. Both houses had three bedrooms and two bathrooms on the upper floor, and each had a den on the main floor. Simply adding a shower to a lower-floor powder room allowed Mittelman and Reese's study to be used as a fourth bedroom. This minor innovation in Mittelman and Reese's smaller homes resulted in housing that cost less to build and sold faster and at higher prices than the larger, 2,000-square-foot homes nearby. Merely adding the shower also eventually opened another door for my firm. The competing developer later hired us and started us on a whole new phase of builder-developer architecture throughout the Bay Area.

At this earlier point, though, adjacent land was still available for further development. Based on Mittelman and Reese's success, the landowner increased the price per acre over what Mittelman and Reese had paid for the first parcel. Mittelman and Reese stubbornly refused to pay more, but another developer with his own architect did. He copied the Mittelman and Reese designs and continued the concept to great prosperity. Ultimately, Mittelman, Reese, and I learned that Silicon Valley was a changing, growing area, and that nothing stayed the same for long. Adjustments, whether in plans or in price, were required, particularly in the rapidly changing arena of real estate. With this lesson in mind, we went on to develop many successful projects together.

Another developer in need of design help was Mike Engdol, a former carpenter who decided to go after the brass ring himself. He secured financing from the same lender as Mittelman and Reese. When he had trouble selling his tract homes, the lender put him in touch with me, largely because I had provided meaningful consultation that helped make Mittelman and Reese successful. The lender had a vested interest in protecting its own investment in Engdol's project and wanted it to be successful as well.

During a walk-through of the homes, I followed Engdol, an imposing man who stood well over six feet tall and weighed 275 pounds, as he lumbered through the house, pounding the floor with his cane. I cringed at the absence of any cohesive design: too-small windows, placed four feet above the floor, were too high for a child to see out and too low to place a dresser beneath—just the opposite of optimal window placement. Realizing late in construction that the small windows left the bedrooms dim, Engdol had patched a window into the interior wall to allow some light from the hall into the bedrooms. To maintain bedroom privacy, these interior windows were made of corrugated glass reminiscent of dental offices in the 1950s. Multiple materials, from metal panels to stone and multicolored cabinets painted various tones that fought

Taking the indoor-outdoor elements from the single-family home to apartment and condominium complexes extended the California lifestyle to multi-family dwellings. We made a special effort to make windows as big as the code would allow, to retain and capitalize on mature trees on the sites, and to use natural materials that helped blend buildings with nature.

Saratoga Oaks, circa 1970

In the early 1970s, we were working for some of the most successful home developers in the rapidly growing Silicon Valley. They all were competitors to Joe Eichler, whose trademark homes populate many Silicon Valley communities, most notably South Palo Alto. Among our clients were Mackey Homes, Brown and Kaufman, Stone and Shulte, and Mardel Homes.

Around this time, Stoneson Development, owner of the Stonestown shopping center in San Francisco, approached me to help develop a unique piece of property in the Saratoga Hills. Their goal was to build a high-density housing development on a steep hillside among heavy trees, and to provide all the services necessary to maintain this project for the convenience of the homeowners. (This, of course, was before hillside zoning ordinances were enacted. Today, Saratoga has one of the strictest zoning codes in the Bay Area and this project would not be possible.)

It required a great deal of skill to fit the structures properly on the slope and among the trees and to have all of the parts of the houses function well. We had to fit seven to eight units per acre on hillside land, working with the grade and the landscape and using retaining walls to help adjust the balance to make the buildings, roads, and landscaping integrate comfortably.

Crane Place, circa 1980

Bella Vista, circa 1989 (above)

Hampton Apartments, circa 1990 (left)

each other, reflected a general lack of aesthetics. I was not enthusiastic about what I saw.

But I went to work for Engdol, putting my best draftsman on the project to develop a new, better-designed housing tract. The result was a fabulous success. Everyone celebrated. Engdol was now rich. But when Engdol proceeded to develop a third tract, the party suddenly was over. The superior draftsman quit my firm. My firm was not offered a new contract with Engdol. A short time later I learned that the draftsman had gone to work directly for Engdol, acing me out of the project altogether. And so I learned another lesson: that while some people are very appreciative of good work, some have very short memories. Our future contracts included clauses that were more protective of my firm's interests and employees.

A very successful and well-known housing developer was Joseph Eichler, who developed his first tract in 1952 in Palo Alto, the Fairmeadow Tract. Although he was not an architect himself, he, like Mittelman and Reese, took the unusual step of employing architects to help him with design, even though the housing demand after World War II was so great that most tract home developers got away with doing without architectural or design expertise. Eichler's concept was well received in Palo Alto. His open-style floor plans appealed to the casual lifestyle that Californians lived. He also included household appliances in each home; the cost of the refrigerator, washer, oven, and other appliances was included in the monthly mortgage payment. This innovative financing step relieved the mostly young homebuyers from following the biggest purchase of their lives with a need to buy thousands of dollars worth of appliances on top of it.

Joe Eichler hired outstanding architects who created unusually modern homes in the 1950s and 1960s. The Eichler houses had flat or slightly pitched tar-and-gravel roofs and wood exteriors. They were built on concrete slabs with radiant heating built into the floors. Open kitchens, dining ells that flowed to a living room area, and floor-to-ceiling windows looking over gardens or patios were hallmarks of the Eichler home, creating a big-house look in a relatively small number of square feet. Few interior walls meant less privacy, but some found the "great room" concept appealing for family life.

Another hallmark of the Eichler home was its extensive use of glass. But while a house with a north-south orientation could enjoy wonderful daylight and garden views, the same house on a lot facing east-west could become stiflingly hot on summer afternoons, when the sun's power is amplified, blazing through large sheets of glass. This is the type of design problems that architects face.

Eichler homes sold quickly in Palo Alto, where Eichler called on the talents of a brilliant young Stanford art professor, Matt Kahn, to accent and accessorize the model homes. Unusual fabrics, colorful touches, and innovative floor coverings made the model homes a three-dimensional art experience. Augmented by creative lighting and sophisticated landscape design, the models were breathtaking—and quite a contrast to the bare, brown-toned houses available for purchase throughout most of the area, which looked out on un-landscaped dirt.

Though the homes sold quickly in Palo Alto, it may be that Eichler's success, which was recognized and promoted by the press with outstanding publications and architectural awards, depended more on location than on design. Built on tracts in Sunnyvale and Santa Clara, the same homes moved much more slowly and brought significantly lower prices than those in Palo Alto, where the public schools are excellent and Stanford is but a bike ride away. Many other builders included Eichler features in their more traditional designs in order to create successful buildings, but these builders did not have the control over large parcels of land in Palo Alto that Eichler did. While design is important, location, as the real estate professionals preach, is most important.

In 1953, Eichler developed the tract that he said was his own favorite, the Greenmeadow tract. Complementing the casual lifestyle that his homes encouraged, this tract featured a central recreation complex, with tennis courts and an Olympic-sized swimming pool, and a private park maintained by the community. California living could be enjoyed even by those of modest means. This project set a tone for future housing developments all over the country.

Living in well-conceived homes improved the lifestyles of the technology employees as well as the industry executives. They realized, after living in highly functional and highly aesthetic places, that architecture was not just a beauty contest, and that evaluating architecture on the basis of style alone is like evaluating a person strictly on looks. The most important aspects—character, functionality, and sensitivity—are ignored. By living in homes that reflected and affected their lifestyle choices, residents began to envision a quality of life that was to become the envy of the world.

Sunset Magazine promulgated this lifestyle, featuring the best of Western living in its pages. In the post-war years, between 1950 and 1980, the influence of *Sunset Magazine* was immeasurable. *Magazine* features included major concept pieces on how to live, with examples ranging from modest to expensive homes and showing everything from hobby rooms to garden gazebos, pools, and decks. Publishing the work of young architects and landscape architects hailing from Washington State to Arizona, *Sunset* contributed to the West Coast style of architecture and Silicon Valley way of life by showcasing the creative ability of a generation to develop great concepts for living well. Books covering subjects from woodworking and landscaping to decking, kitchens, and bathrooms were published under the *Sunset* imprimatur.

Builder-developers picked up on the features in *Sunset*'s pages and incorporated them into otherwise traditional homes, demonstrating that the *Sunset* quality of life could be captured even for those who dismissed the modern California architecture that the magazine so often touted. Traditional homes in California could have larger windows, more exterior doors, patios, and decks, for example, to make use of the climatic and visual advantages of

Northern California. People who were not ready to embrace the unique features of modern architecture could still adopt the unique qualities of California living by adapting the ideas in *Sunset*'s pages.

Times change. Today *Sunset* is owned by a large, East Coast–based media empire that has lost the vision of the regionally oriented founding publishers, Bill and Mel Lane. The magazine no longer conveys the many advantages that this milder, insect-free climate allows for the homeowner. As a result, the architectural character of the region has been diluted. Without a magazine to communicate the Western lifestyle, newcomers build houses here like the ones back home. And the magazine that chronicled the region has become another national general-interest publication.

While some developers chose to focus on residential development to provide housing for the many employees whom industry was hiring, others chose commercial development. Although the returns were greater in industrial development, so were the risks. With residential projects, a developer could always drop the price and sell for a little bit less. But if commercial developers' buildings didn't rent, they were in a bind as to how to pay off their high-interest land and construction loans. They needed capital and staying power to outlast a down market.

Still, the lines between residential and commercial development were beginning to blur, with some developers delving into both enterprises. An architectural change that would redefine the Silicon Valley workplace was in the offing.

If living in well-conceived homes improved the lifestyles of the technology employees, it certainly had a tremendous impact on the industry executives, the most visionary of whom saw an application for California design in the workplace. By living in homes that reflected and affected their lifestyle choices, a few executives connected the dots to conceive of a workplace that could foster interaction, cooperation, and creativity—and positively affect the bottom line.

Earlier office buildings consisted mainly of rectangular offices of varying sizes. The more important the employee, the larger the office he was assigned. Long corridors with four-sided rooms lining either side were the norm. Exteriors were designed to make imposing statements. Banks, capitols, and other public buildings reflected the great empires, mimicking the style of Greek temples, Renaissance churches, or Roman columns. Little consideration was given to the functions taking place inside these buildings.

This model began to change in the Santa Clara Valley in the mid-1950s. At Ampex Corporation, President George Long and Chief Operating Officer Robert Sackman both had worked with me to design their own custom homes. In a first step toward innovation, they realized the importance of their executive assistants, especially in the midst of heated meetings or phone calls, when information might need to be retrieved at a moment's notice. Configuring new office space so that the executive could always be in eye contact with the executive assistant saved many an Ampex executive's skin. The executive had only to tap a pencil or make some other gesture to signal that help was needed to deal with a situation taking place on the phone or in the office.

A bigger step forward in corporate design was taken at ROLM Corporation. Ken Oshman, the "O" in ROLM and the company's president, also had contracted my services to create a large and elegant home for his family. Oshman had recently graduated from Stanford's School of Engineering and was forward-thinking and innovative. ROLM's mission was nothing short of taking on the nation's major phone companies. In the 1970s, Oshman and his partners foresaw a revolutionary expansion of the use of telephones and telephone lines, conceiving of unheard-of services that are now run-of-the-mill: voice mail, call waiting, call forwarding, faxes, and complete records on all calls, including time and date, who made them, and who received them. In the business place, access codes would help control costs by controlling who could make long-distance calls.

When the company purchased 41 acres in San Jose and set out to develop 400,000 square feet, the partners were every bit as imaginative as they were in envisioning the future of telephone services. In addition to engineering offices and manufacturing space, they wanted to develop an extensive dining center and a physical fitness center for employees. Although I had not designed commercial buildings in California, Oshman asked me to submit a bid. Of the fifteen firms that vied for the ROLM job, I was the only one without industrial experience. In this case, it worked to my benefit.

Successful designers reworked previously successful plans in their presentations to new clients. Without a similar project to work from, I was free to present the kind of building that I would design from scratch if I won the bid. I described my vision of California living, applying the residential model to the workplace as I painted a picture of integrating indoor and outdoor space for maximum enjoyment and utilization. I addressed security issues not with locks and alarms but with pools of water and landscaping that limited unauthorized access. I devised an economically feasible air-conditioning system for buildings with operable windows and glass doors. My series of sketches reflected the innovative philosophy and principles of the ROLM business plan itself.

Somewhat amazingly, I got the job.

The ROLM campus that I ultimately designed was composed of four buildings: two for engineering and manufacturing, one for dining, and one for athletics. Together with the space around and between them, they created an ambience conducive to interaction, interdependence, and integration. Cars circled the outer ring of the campus and were parked in quadrants near the buildings, a comfortable walk away from the destination points and out of the way of those on the campus. Gateways from the parking lots, between the buildings, led to a Shangri-la in the middle of the campus, from which each building could be entered. Green belts and ponds and waterfalls created a Japanese garden effect. Lawns doubled as playing fields for employees' touch football or soccer games. On Friday afternoons, the lawns became beer gardens as employees kicked back to relax and celebrate the oncoming weekend.

Instead of a standard cafeteria, I developed a dining complex built on a square with multilevel indoor and outdoor eating spaces that could be partitioned off into private dining rooms for presentations or work group lunch meetings. A "scatter" kitchen allowed employees to go straight to the station they wanted without waiting in long cafeteria lines in which every patron walked by every menu item. Innovative in its time, this concept has become a mainstay of Silicon Valley's corporate cafeterias.

Wrapped by decks and surrounded by lake systems, with skylights spilling sun between peaked roofs, the building reflected an appreciation for aesthetics and an acknowledgment that lunch could be more than a sandwich; it could be a respite, an opportunity to recharge one's batteries.

The work at ROLM was productivity-focused. As long as employees accomplished what they needed to, they were free to take time off during the day for a leisurely lunch, a walk, or a workout at the company's athletic facility, which included an Olympic-sized swimming pool, a track, a gym, billiards, ping pong, and even hot tubs.

Engineering offices were set up as incubators of creativity. Small conference areas between office clusters led to cross-pollination of ideas. An engineer could stroll out of his office, bump into a colleague and bounce an idea or two off him and enjoy a social interaction. Conference rooms were flexible: they could be set up as theaters-in-the-round or as lecture halls facing a white board, or be focused around a projected image. Many conference rooms were built on piers projecting over ponds, with peaceful, calming views that created a retreat-like feeling for employees meeting in them.

Man-made lakes flowed from outdoors to inside, where they burst into fountains. The gurgle of the bubbling water, the indoor planting, and the glass completed the indoor-outdoor, California-style architecture as applied to the workplace.

The result was the transformation of corporation to community. A unique spirit developed at ROLM, a spirit of companionship, collegiality, friendship, and mental stimulation. The place lent itself to lingering, to dreaming. Employees no longer ran for the doors at the five o'clock whistle. The architecture of mood, emotion, and feeling created a gigantic workshop, in which people enjoyed the creativity that they were allowed, where work was cooperative, dress was casual, and the lines between work and leisure blurred.

I like to think that the chance that Oshman took on me paid off. Choosing my fresh creativity over experience and reputation allowed ROLM to distinguish itself early from the other technology companies, both in its plant design and ultimately, in the way that work was done, in the way that employees were treated, and in the priority employees gave to their work. If the ROLM campus became a model for the Silicon Valley workplace, the risk tolerance there soon became a mantra for Silicon Valley success.

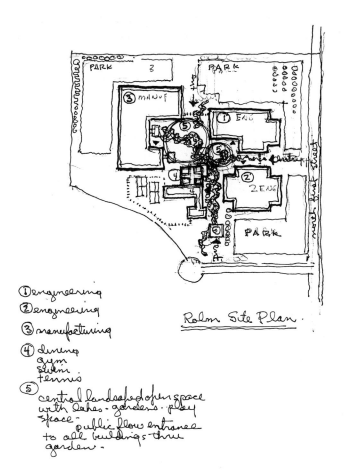

① engineering
② engineering
③ manufacturing
④ dining
   gym
   swim
   tennis
⑤ central landscaped open space
   with lakes - gardens - play
   space - public flow entrance
   to all buildings thru
   garden.

Rolm Site Plan.

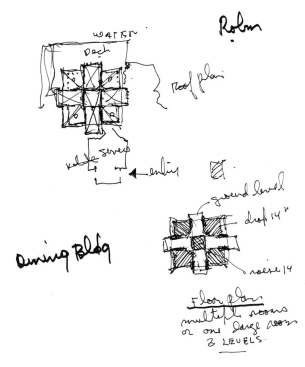

Rolm

Dining Bldg

ROLM Corporation, circa 1982

ROLM Corporation was on the cutting edge of industrial development. It was patterned after the indoor-outdoor living style of California's residential architecture, an architecture that could only be implemented in a friendly, mild climate.

This group of pictures includes dining facilities, engineering offices, and manufacturing space. ROLM's campus set a standard for Silicon Valley. It featured large, open areas where beer busts were held on Friday afternoons and where employees could enjoy lunch on a weekday or plan work projects. The environment was designed to encourage communication.

The small lakes created a sense of tranquility. We projected conference rooms out onto the lake, or, in other cases, we brought the lake in under the building, so that glass-walled executive offices floated over the water. The dining building, with its patios, also had a special relationship to water and the landscaped gardens. The window-walls literally opened up, and the inside of the building became indistinguishable from the outside. You could be totally inside and feel as though you were standing outside under a covered deck.

The buildings housed all the functions of a standard-issue workplace. The difference was that this building complex was wrapped around a garden. The buildings' entrances faced the courtyard-like garden so that only after entering the garden could you move on into the workplace. The buildings themselves were California buildings—light, airy spaces where communication between offices was the norm.

ROLM Corporation, circa 1982

SCI Manufacturing Corporation, circa 1990

Another example of residential-to-industrial design was SCI Manufacturing Corporation, where trellises, sprawling lawns, and prominent stairways overlooking green gardens typify the architectural style that was founded in Silicon Valley.

The Steinberg Group, circa 1997

The Steinberg Group office features an inviting, residential-style entryway without forfeiting the functional work spaces necessary for a busy architectural firm.

By 1975, Silicon Valley was taking off in full force. Technological advances, some spawning whole new industries, were coming fast and furious, as they continue to today, dramatically altering the look and feel of the Santa Clara Valley. The once agriculturally based, day-laborer community not only looked different physically, with corporate campuses replacing open farmland; it was becoming a place where hierarchies were flattening out, where shared employer-employee responsibility was becoming the norm, and where values had a prominent role in workplace policies and interactions.

With effectiveness measured by productivity rather than the hours spent wedded to the desk, high-technology employees felt comfortable taking the time for recreation in the middle of their day, running or lifting weights with friends, sharing lunch with a spouse, or ducking out for parent-teacher conferences. They knew that they could come back to work in the evenings or on weekends to finish what they needed to, and that they would find others doing the same.

In order to build this kind of commitment to the corporate team, companies in Silicon Valley embraced the personal needs of their employees. In addition to flexible work schedules and increasingly, the opportunity to work from home, some offered generous maternity and paternity leave programs; some offered on-site infant and toddler day-care centers. Staff development courses and sabbatical leave were adopted from academe to enhance the work lives of employees. Many companies added tuition reimbursement programs and stock option incentives, offering employees the chance to profit from their own initiative and industriousness by giving them a piece of the corporate pie. Entire books have been written on the now-famous "H-P Way," which pioneered this symbiosis of mutual respect, trust, responsibility, and reward.

On the political side, the City of San Jose was making great efforts to attract and maintain a vibrant business community. Mayor Susan Hammer did for corporations what the corporations did for their employees: she initiated and implemented programs to attract and retain them.

Upon her election, Hammer, a former San Jose City Council member and long-time resident, saw former Mayor Tom McEnery's pet project—downtown redevelopment—being fulfilled. She turned her attention to the "tentacles" that Dutch Hamann had created and left largely ignored some four decades earlier. While McEnery's legacy was rebuilding the physical heart of the city, Hammer concerned herself with the human heart. She cared deeply about the city's sense of dignity, about public safety, schools, and, to fuel her

6

vision, economic development. She knew that a healthy economy would fund the programs that she wanted to grow, so her first focus was on bringing and maintaining business in San Jose.

Hammer, like her predecessor, was well aware of the importance of maintaining a solid industrial base. For years, Tom McEnery had courted major corporations to locate and maintain their headquarters in downtown San Jose, both for business development purposes and to give the city an important identity. In addition, both Hammer and McEnery wanted to ensure against industry leaving town and taking local jobs with them. So they carefully guarded against any civic arrogance that could ultimately lead to corporate exodus, labor shortages, and future community problems.

Hammer met with city staff twice a week to discuss service to the business community. She expedited building permits, and like her predecessor, brought sidewalks, sewers, and utilities to the city outskirts, where companies were building, and made a routine of personally phoning corporate executives to find out what they needed from the city in order to thrive. Like a sales rep covering a customer list, Hammer showered the business community with personal attention, wooing business leaders to establish their companies within San Jose's city limits.

As a small company needing to expand, Cisco Systems was being courted by other cities, including Seattle and Salt Lake City. Had Mayors Hayes, McEnery, and their predecessors not built the necessary infrastructure years before, Hammer would not have been positioned to persuade Cisco to stay in San Jose. She eased the building permit process for Cisco and, along with other expedited processes, convinced the company to expand in Silicon Valley.

Hammer also made an all-out effort to get Adobe Systems to build in downtown San Jose, bringing thousands of jobs to the area and generating the tax revenues necessary to fund her social and anticrime programs.

Hammer believed that the strength of the city depended on healthy schools and neighborhoods. When she took office, the economy was depressed, and she knew that she had to develop economic resources in a hurry if she wanted to have an impact on the city. Thus, Hammer went on record as supporting the city's card rooms—often seedy, smoke-filled nightclubs in which legal gambling took place, as well as possible illegal activities. Once the city developed the funds it needed, card rooms fell out of favor, with headlines screaming for their closure. But at the time, the city was desperate for money to fund its improvement programs, and card rooms, though subject to criticism, provided a legal revenue source.

Gangs were prominent, both in the schools and on the streets. Schools were lacking in infrastructure. So, after economic development, her next order of business was to take the money generated by her efforts to bring business to San Jose and create an anti-gang program. School officials and police worked together to combat illegal gang activities; the high-technology sector donated computers to schools in order to engage kids in computer learning and thus diffuse interest in gangs; and the Hammer administration built 150 after-school homework centers throughout the city. In addition, San Jose became the first city in the United States to wire its schools, kindergarten through high school, for the Internet. Challenging the business community to match its $1 million contribution three-to-one, the city raised $4 million for the project. Other Silicon Valley cities soon followed suit.

Hammer also instituted the "green line," a band around the parts of the city where her administration wanted industry to develop. Beyond this "green line," city services such as sewers, sidewalks, and utilities would not be provided. Encouraging companies to rehabilitate run-down areas of the city achieved the twin goals of limiting urban sprawl and cleaning up shabby neighborhoods. Meanwhile, high-density housing corridors were developed along transportation lines.

Encouraging business to contribute to the community resulted not only in the decline of gang-related activity and improved technology in schools. It also had farther-reaching results: San Jose dropped to one of the lowest homicide rates per capita in the country.

Just as Hammer encouraged business to participate in the broader community, so businesses empowered their employees—through trust and responsibility—to get involved in the life of their communities. The initiative to build institutions that would enhance the community, fueled not only by tax revenues that valley companies generated but also by corporate matching philanthropy programs and support from corporate foundations, helped create an unparalleled quality of life in Silicon Valley.

Innovation, it seemed, was contagious, traversing from the Silicon Valley workplace to its municipalities, schools, and religious institutions.

The story of Cupertino's Guided Learning Center tells a tale of transferring business innovation into the public school arena. The bright young families in this public school district demanded excellence in public education. When the Cupertino School District found itself in need of a new superintendent of schools, it looked north to San Francisco and recruited Yvette del Prado, an experienced teacher who had the political know-how and the necessary support of minority constituents to implement radical change from the status quo. Her founding principle was this: that schools must be built on the premise of "kids first." While teachers wanted their lounge to be a haven away from the demands of students, del Prado wanted just the opposite. Her vision would place the teachers' lounge in the middle of the school's most high-traffic area, where teachers would be accessible to answer students' questions even at break times.

Adopting the multidisciplinary approach already prominent in colleges and universities and adapted by the high-technology workplace, del Prado worked to configure a school building that would facilitate a fully integrated curriculum, engaging students on every level, from academics to art to music education. She dubbed it the Guided Learning Center.

Twenty years earlier, in 1959, radiologist Henry Kaplan was influenced by the same kind of thinking when he led the campaign to move the Stanford Medical Center to the main campus from San Francisco. He saw the collaboration that Dean Frederick Terman was initiating between the School of

Engineering and other schools within the university. Fruitful marriages between business and engineering, and between the basic sciences and engineering, led Kaplan to believe that prospects were good for interdisciplinary interaction between medicine and engineering, if only the geographical distance between San Francisco and Palo Alto could be bridged. In addition, Kaplan was concerned that the medical students Stanford was turning out were too insular, too focused on their own profession. Sharing a campus with Stanford's six other professional and graduate schools would broaden the doctors' education. Exposure to the humanities, engineering, education, sciences, law, and business would produce more well-rounded members of the medical profession, Kaplan believed. Finally, the other schools would benefit, too, Kaplan thought, from the opportunities for cross-pollination that an on-campus medical school would offer.

Already thinking in a collaborative mode, Kaplan set out to engage an architect to design a world-class medical center on the Stanford campus. He cast his eye east, hoping to interest prominent architect Edward Durell Stone to design the project. Examples of Stone's work include the original Museum of Modern Art in New York, the U.S. Embassy in New Delhi, the U.S. Pavilion at the Brussels World's Fair, the General Motors Building in New York City, the National Geographic Building in Washington, D.C., and the Kennedy Center for the Performing Arts, also in Washington, D.C. Just one hospital, Kaplan knew, would not be enough to draw someone as renowned as Stone. But a hospital, a city hall, and several libraries might entice him to come west and open an office. Working with City of Palo Alto leadership to create a package of projects to make the travel worth Stone's while, Kaplan was able to persuade Stone to come set up shop in Palo Alto. It wasn't long before medical students were mixing it up with engineers, business students, and lawyers on the main Stanford campus near Palo Alto, where they could explore any number of subjects in addition to their own.

In Cupertino, the Guided Learning Center's architecture also put the world of knowledge at a student's fingertips. In this state-of-the-art school, the multipurpose room that served as gymnasium, auditorium, and rainy-day lunchroom was the middle of the campus. Classrooms wrapped its perimeter. A library opened onto this large, central room from the back; a computer room and a music room opened onto it from either side. The campus also included a dance studio, a woodshop, and an art room. True to her vision, Yvette del Prado made sure that the teachers' lounge was right in the middle of the campus.

On such a campus, students were all but propelled into the computer room or the library. The tools at their immediate disposal easily answered whatever curiosity struck them. When, for example, the students studied Shakespeare, they studied all aspects of Shakespeare and his plays. In the library, they read the plays and studied history; in the music room, they learned period pieces. Costumes were part of the art curriculum and lighting and technical aspects were part of the science program. It was an innovative and multidisciplinary way to teach and learn, placing "kids first," as del Prado had intended. What made it possible was thinking outside the box when it came to the configuration of the school building itself.

Later, del Prado went on to work in the high-technology arena herself. She spent time at Tandem Computers and Silicon Graphics, Inc. She also chaired the fundraising effort for The Tech Museum of Innovation in San Jose, which was begun in 1994.

Yvette Del Prado demonstrated that the physical components of a school contribute to the quality of the education it delivers and affect the institution's image of itself as well as the image it broadcasts to its community. A school with inconsistent campus design and unappealing buildings transmits a message about itself no matter how accomplished its student body.

Another case in point is Bellarmine High School, which in the 1970s was a Jesuit campus lacking in aesthetics. Its programs were nothing short of excellent: its debate program bred champions; its math and science programs were world-renowned; it placed students in the top universities in the country. But there was a disconnect between the quality of the education and the environment in which it took place.

When the high school put out a request for architects to be interviewed for a new science building, an alumnus encouraged the administration to talk to me. The alumnus, a personal contact who had been helpful to my career, was active in the San Jose community. It behooved me to follow through on his effort to win me a hearing. So, although one of the half-dozen architects interviewed already had done extensive work for the school and was very likely to get the job, I agreed to talk to the priest in charge and his committee. What did I have to lose but an hour?

Something about walking through that campus, where such intellectual excellence was bred, and where the physical layout was such a hodgepodge, inspired me to get on my soapbox. Since the Renaissance, the Catholic community has been a leader in intellectual and creative development, I told the priest who was interviewing me. The Medici family played a strong role in world history and in the way that the modern mind has evolved, and their background and interest was architecture, I said. Yet over time, so many fine institutions have become just buildings, or just campuses, without a lot of thought given to consistency in design and function.

This was incongruous, I said, particularly in a Catholic institution, where excellence is the standard. Teaching and communication could be terrifically enhanced through architecture, I said. Architecture is a problem-solution game, and if well thought through, attention to architecture can address many campus problems, logistical and otherwise. If I were hired to design a science building, I would do far more than that, I said. I would take a fresh look at all of the building sites, relandscape, reorient the campus so that parking is not the first thing seen by someone entering the grounds, all in an effort to develop students' pride in and through their surroundings.

With a Jewish surname and a critical voice, not to mention the existence

Guided Learning Center, Cupertino
Unified School District, circa 1988

The innovative plan for the Guided Learning
Center in Cupertino reflects the vision of
Superintendent Yvette del Prado to put
"kids first."

Carney Science Center, Bellarmine College Preparatory School, circa 1989

Development of the Carney Science Center at Bellarmine combined teaching goals with campus aesthetics for a building both highly functional and visually attractive.

Santa Clara County Children's Shelter, circa 1990

Santa Clara County is and was responsible for taking care of abused children who needed protection, not only from abusers from the outside world but also, after they were brought into the county's jurisdiction, from bullies who could harm them in their new environment.

Since the shelter's most important objective was to safeguard the children's well-being, as its architects we had to provide many spaces within the building and on the grounds where children could get away from each other and engage in a range of activities. A playing field, a volleyball court, a shuffleboard game, quiet reading areas, and private spots were built into the plan from the outset. In addition, the shelter required separate sleeping quarters according to the children's age and gender.

We accomplished these objectives with a series of cottages overlooking a large central

playing field. Many small pockets of space surrounded the site's periphery. In addition, there was an administration building, dining building, and gymnasium.

Within the individual cottages, the county required that a variety of spaces be created for watching television, reading, and playing. Each child needed privacy, but the county also needed to be able to observe each child unobtrusively. We wanted to create an atmosphere that was comfortable, warm, and friendly without compromising security. Our goal was to provide a delightful, beautiful environment that would bring out the best in its residents.

Before starting this project, we visited many projects in other counties, and we observed that the victimized children in some of those counties were treated as though they were criminals. The staff at Santa Clara County made it absolutely clear that this orientation was unacceptable.

of a viable inside candidate, I never anticipated getting the job. Yet, two hours after I returned to my office, I received a call from the priest in charge: I was hired.

I never had more fun than I did working with the Jesuits to design the Carney Science Building. The outer ring was classroom and lab space, with the teachers' offices in the back of each, abutting one another. This allowed the teachers, who were situated in the middle of the building, to interact and build on each others' ideas. Stargazing features were incorporated into the roof, and animal labs were designed for safety and effectiveness.

Over time, I also helped to remodel many of Bellarmine's older buildings, cleaning house so that the campus could function effectively for the future. A swimming pool was sited and installed and recently, a new chapel was designed and built.

Just as a school's buildings speak volumes about the institution itself, a community's public buildings—both their location and their design—tell a lot about its self-image and priorities.

When Dianne McKenna was elected to the Santa Clara County Board of Supervisors in 1985, her priority was the county children's shelter. But as is often the case in public service, the urgent supersedes the important; as McKenna entered office, budget challenges persisted, and issues with the county jail pushed her priority to the back burner.

The jail issue pitted a jail consultant and the county sheriff, both of whom advocated one inmate per cell, against the supervisors, who believed that greater density was possible and that it would relieve pressure on the budget. The consultant advocated for a new jail in a new location; the supervisors believed that the current jail, with its existing underground tunnels to the county courthouse for trial, could be adapted to meet current needs. The conflict became so heated that it wound up in court, and the judge, who agreed with the consultant and the sheriff, threatened to fine and jail the supervisors themselves unless they commissioned a new jail in Milpitas. Ultimately, the supervisors prevailed, but not without constant, focused attention on McKenna's part.

Once the jail issue was resolved, McKenna was freer to pursue her own agenda. Like others, McKenna found the county children's shelter utterly inadequate for its intended purpose of providing a safe haven for children whose parents were not competent to raise them. When I was called in to review the site, my first impression was of two little girls playing happily together while a third sat not far from them, sobbing and ignored. There was no private space where this sad child could express her feelings. The building had one large main room with sleeping rooms around the perimeter, limited outdoor play space, and worst of all, it was in a dilapidated neighborhood. The facility could not satisfy the multiple needs of children who had been neglected and abused. Children were thrown together in inappropriate mixes of age and gender, some receiving the same type of abuse from older children that they had received at home.

There was a clear need for a new and more sensitive shelter. Without one, the county was not upholding its responsibility to protect children.

McKenna mapped out a plan for a new shelter that would be funded half by the private sector and half by the county. While she focused on securing financial commitments from various public entities, her husband, Silicon Valley marketing guru extraordinaire Regis McKenna, solicited the private funds necessary to build the new shelter. Dianne McKenna convinced builders and developers to participate in the project by giving donations and reducing their fees.

We had been working with county staff leaders from the children's shelter. Staff members like Nancy Wiener devoted their lives to caring for others. She and the other staff leaders had been striving for years to improve the facility. They needed space in a nice neighborhood where some love and dignity could be translated into kindness and caring. My firm was a part of the team already in place when Dianne and her board of building developers were ready to proceed with development of a safe, comfortable home for approximately one hundred children ages 6 through 16. We were invited to continue as the architects. In addition, we were asked to design a large nursery for younger children, where they could be treated medically and cared for until they were placed in private homes.

Seven cottages are laid out around the perimeter of the new shelter. Each sleeps about fifteen children of similar ages and the same gender, in bedrooms built for two. The cottages are built around a large, grassy playing field. An administration building includes areas for supervised visits with parents. There are separate entrances for victimized children and for parents who may be the cause of the trauma. A dining facility and infirmary are also included on the ten-acre site. And although the nearby residents at first complained of a children's shelter being built in their neighborhood, the supervisors, especially McKenna, were able to convince them that this could be a win-win situation for the county's children and for the neighborhood.

McKenna also put energy into the programs offered by the shelter. She instituted an artist-in-residence program, a Head Start–type preschool program, a recreation program, and cultural activities that offered the children hope for their own futures. During her tenure on the Board of Supervisors, McKenna also established Kids in Common, a program that linked people who needed resources with those who have resources. Again, it was an unusual marriage of public and private sectors that was able to accomplish a lot for the health of the county's children. For example, while only 66 percent of two-year-olds nationwide are immunized, Kids in Common was able to raise that figure to 95 percent in Santa Clara County.

McKenna's other accomplishments included maintaining low-density housing in the hills, despite increasing budget pressure to broaden the tax base with higher-density housing; completion of Highway 85, linking U.S. 101 and Interstate 280; completion of Highway 237, which traverses the bottom of the bay, linking San Jose to the East Bay; and creating a separate county transit board, which would allow Santa Clara a better chance of hiring an outstanding executive to run its transit programs. Previously, the transit director reported not only to the board of supervisors, but also to the county executive. This made it difficult to attract a top-notch transit executive, who might not want to work under another county employee.

A final footnote about the high regard that accrued to McKenna as a result of her outstanding public service: when the United Way of Santa Clara failed in the late 1990s, the leadership sought out a philanthropist who had the ability and effectiveness to raise millions of dollars to revive the agency. They specifically sought Dianne McKenna, who immediately solicited a number of successful Silicon Valley executives to help bail out United Way. Steve Kirsch, who was young and relatively new to Silicon Valley, was a key member of the committee, and he volunteered to contribute the first $1 million. That donation was the catalyst that helped McKenna successfully rescue United Way.

Another celebrated project, The Tech Museum of Innovation in San Jose, is a metaphor for the evolving image that San Jose has struggled to develop for itself.

The story begins some twenty years before the Tech Museum was built, and it begins not in San Jose, but in the North County city of Palo Alto. There, the Junior League began interviewing architects for a museum that would tell the Silicon Valley story and feature the latest advances in technology fields. The Junior League wanted the museum to be located in North County, and they wanted an architect of world acclaim to design it. While San Jose was viewing itself as the heart of Silicon Valley, those in the North County looked down at San Jose as tasteless and unrefined. They felt better suited to handle the important work of building a monument to the industry that had earned the valley its name, and they pursued internationally renowned architect Ricardo Legoretta to design it.

A bidding war ensued over the Tech Museum, with various Silicon Valley cities offering different degrees of financial participation and support. In the desire to rebuild San Jose, redevelopment advocates Tom McEnery, later mayor of San Jose, and *San Jose Mercury News* publisher Anthony P. Ridder, now president of Knight Ridder Corporation, were visionary and relentless in leading the charge to build the museum in San Jose as a cultural anchor. Together, they persuaded the city to donate land along the Guadalupe River Park for both the Tech Museum and a new children's museum.

During the economic downturn of the 1970s, when the business community largely focused on its own corporate work and not on the museum, plans lagged. Meanwhile, though, the children's museum proponents had already organized a board of directors, they had a chief executive officer in place, and they had successfully raised the funds to initiate their project, which was intended to be housed in a secondary building on the Guadalupe River Park site. This being the case, the city determined that Legoretta should be the chief architect for the children's museum as well as the Tech Museum, for consistent and complementary design.

With light-rail tracks now wrapping the Guadalupe River Park property, and the river blocking public access on one side, siting the buildings required a thoughtful, long-term perspective. Placing the Children's Discovery Museum on the corner of the site blocked traffic circulation and rendered the rest of the property all but unusable for another public building—let alone a building that was supposed to have been the centerpiece of the development.

The children's museum building has an unusual form. The main exhibition hall is long and narrow like a corridor, restricting circulation. The skinny, rectangular shape, with a plate-glass window on one of the long sides, limits display space to a single wall. A narrow stairway and dark, low ceilings under the balconies limit the types of exhibits that can be installed on the main floor. The upper level of the museum is difficult to reach, it is too big to be intimate, and it is too small for large displays. Also, without the level of scrutiny that was being imposed on the Tech Museum, problems of water leakage, utility, and design had inadvertently been built into the Children's Discovery Museum.

When Tom McEnery, who was already engaged in revitalizing downtown San Jose, became mayor, he was quick to recognize the Children's Discovery Museum's planning problems and how the building choked off access to the proposed Tech Museum site. Rather than trying to work with the unworkable, McEnery, along with Frank Taylor and the redevelopment agency, came up with a new, downtown location for the Tech Museum.

While the location has been an important factor in the success of the Tech Museum, project scrutiny and oversight is a close second. No less than eight architects were involved in various aspects of its design. Legoretta remained the design architect responsible for the general appearance of the building, and he came up with a breathtaking exterior. The museum hired two architects to oversee the function of the exhibits. The redevelopment agency, which had put up a large sum of money and was responsible for the budget and for design consistency within the heart of the city, hired two other architects to keep watch on the city's interests. An Imax theater architect, a dining facility architect, a retail store architect, and an interior designer all were on board for pieces of the project. And all had different—and sometimes competing—interests to protect. While the children's museum had suffered from lack of project management, the threat to the Tech Museum was an excess of experts. The tension among all the architects plus the graphic designers and exhibit designers, who all together constituted a high-powered group with great ability and large egos, eventually led the mayor to hire me at the front-end of the process as coordinating architect.

Because of the problems associated with the children's museum, I was charged with responsibility for project management, including the coordination of consultants and architects. The role I played was less being a boss than being a team coach, trying to bring out the best in each player. I already had a successful track record on civic projects, including the complicated restoration of the county's historic but tired and earthquake-damaged courthouse, just down the street from the Tech Museum's new downtown site.

The Tech Museum of Innovation, circa 1996

The dome erupting over a mango cube identifies downtown San Jose's visual centerpiece, The Tech Museum of Innovation. The finished museum is the combined work of a dozen design professionals with various and sometimes conflicting purposes. I served as "team captain," coordinating the designers' many interests into one cohesive museum.

The courthouse was built of unreinforced masonry. In a region plagued by earthquakes, it had suffered considerable damage. The 1989 Loma Prieta earthquake finally forced its closure, and the courts were moved to temporary quarters while the future of the courthouse was weighed. For two years, the historic courthouse sat idle as the legal community and historians demanded its restoration and fiscal conservatives demanded that minimal funds be expended to develop additional courtroom space. The new county executive, Sally Reed, found herself in the middle of a political battle as historic groups rallied around the judges and lawyers to demand that the building be saved, while taxpayers' rights groups advocated a cheaper solution.

In addition to substantial earthquake damage, the courthouse's heating, plumbing, and electrical systems all were in need of upgrade, if not replacement. Yet retrofitting from the interior of the building to preserve the historic exterior was expensive, and no one knew what surprises they might find when they opened up the hundred-year-old walls. It would be much easier to estimate costs accurately and to control the budget on a new building.

The interior of the building was funky. Over the years, each judge had personalized his courtroom to make it his own. One judge, by the name of Joseph Kelly, had decided years earlier that he wanted his courtroom painted kelly green. And so it was. To top him, another judge decided that if Kelly could have a green courtroom, he wanted a red one. Red velvet lined his courtroom walls. Other eccentric personal touches, in judges' chambers, for example, were inconsistent with the historic quality of the building. And yet, the preservationists persisted and the judges wanted to keep their courthouse. Newcomer Reed had no choice but to accede to their wishes, but still she was faced with the pressure to contain costs as tight budgets and fiscally conservative leaders also imposed their will on the process.

In a melding of public- and private-sector professionals, Reed utilized her best strength: delegating difficult tasks to people she believed she could depend on and giving them the leeway to do their jobs. She called in my firm, The Steinberg Group. We had been involved in a number of high-profile projects in the community, and, most importantly, we were well known to be accurate data collectors. We, in turn, brought in expert subcontractors who opened walls and analyzed the scope of the work. Metal workers, masons, sheet-rockers, carpenters, painters, plumbers, electricians, and every class of specialty contractor were called on to offer the competitive bids required in public projects. In the end, the budget was anticipated at $18 million.

Reed's staff worked hand-in-hand with us, writing contracts that both met state requirements and allowed the flexibility necessary to get the right subcontractors for each aspect of the job. It was not the normal government bidding process. It was very creative—but legal! Cost-overruns were a major concern, so contractors were held to their bids, yet the structure also allowed the county to change orders if it chose to do so. Reed's team exemplified professionalism and leadership in working within the framework of rigid county contracts in an unconventional manner. Their work was comparable to that of the most flexible private corporation as they cooperated to satisfy the preservationists, the community, and the judges who would occupy the restored historic building.

The chief judge, Conrad Rushing, worked diligently to win the judges' approval of interior aesthetics that were consistent from one courtroom to the next. While the judges would eventually move on to other jurisdictions or retire, the courtrooms would remain. No more kelly green; no more red velvet. Instead, the courtrooms were painted a restful shade of ivory with soft green and gray-blue trim, the fixtures reflected a historic influence, and the trims and moldings were consistent with the age of the building. In the end, the old courthouse was transformed to one with all the modern comforts and functions but all the charm and dignity of a historic public building. Total cost: $13 million—approximately $5 million less than anticipated.

Just as I had on the county courthouse project, I established control over the Tech Museum's many design professionals slowly, with patience and respect for all team members' ideas, steering the team toward consensus rather than ruling with a heavy hand. It was my job to weigh and balance the inevitable competing interests, and to synthesize conflicting ideas while retaining individual energy, enthusiasm, and creativity for the project. For example, exhibit designers wanted a simple, black box with total flexibility for their exhibits, while Legoretta wanted long, interesting views up, down, and across museum spaces, which limited the exhibit designers. All the while, the redevelopment agency concerned itself with the budget, how the museum might be used for fundraising events that would contribute to museum income, and how the building looked in the context of other buildings on the street. Furthermore, each individual architect had his own particular interest that could have had a negative impact on the others. Our goal was to get the right balance.

Issues of flow and circulation were passed on to Legoretta, who was in Mexico, even though some of the professionals wanted to make these decisions themselves in the interest of saving time. It was important to us as administrators to make sure that Legoretta make the major decisions pertaining to the aesthetics of the building, to ensure that the committees and other architects participated actively in decisions regarding its function, and that we got the best result from the combination of people involved.

In addition, the City of San Jose required a work of art be incorporated in all public projects. To this end, the redevelopment agency invited the head of the arts commission to participate in the project. Now, most artists create their pieces and sell them to public entities expecting that they will be prominently displayed. We, on the other hand, were concerned with finding an appropriate piece of art that neither overwhelmed nor conflicted with the museum itself. The prominence of the art and its function in a technology museum proved to be an additional challenge.

Even with the tremendous numbers of interests and people involved, the Tech Museum has been an immense success—thoughtful, well-designed, and well-received. Corporate participation, in the form of financial backing, programming, and support of the educational enterprise, is high; the fin-

Santa Clara County Courthouse, circa 1992

Restoration of the stately Santa Clara County Courthouse combined the talents of county staff and community members who were determined to bring in the project on time and on budget. Incorporating finishes, colors, and moldings that were consistent with the building's 1890 date of origin represented the consensus opinion of judges, architects, and contractors as well as county officials. The calm and elegance of the finished product are counterpoints to the Tech Museum, which stands just across the plaza in downtown San Jose.

ished product is a strong statement of community, underscoring a dedication to education, youth programming, and interdisciplinary training.

I was proud to be part of the team that designed San Jose's showplace museum, not only because of the quality of the work, but also because of my commitment to this community. When we came to the Bay Area after the war, we were strangers, as were so many of our contemporaries. Our neighbors, who came from a diversity of regions and backgrounds, were determined to make connections and build community. My work on the Tech Museum, the county courthouse, the Mountain View police and fire administration building, and other civic projects helped me to feel that I was a contributing member of my community, bringing my professional expertise to build a region in which my family and other families could flourish. I believe that an architect can find greater personal fulfillment and a better quality of life by concentrating his work in a community rather than diluting himself with major projects over great distances.

Work connections helped us to build a life for ourselves, but they were only a start. We also joined many community organizations and took active roles in them in an effort to meet people and to construct a solid social life for ourselves and our children. The Bay Area lent itself to family and social recreation. We took many jaunts to the beach, where we threw the football around, studied the tide pools, barbecued supper, and enjoyed one another's company. At a memorable and moving family visit to the beach, we were joined by a busload of inner-city children making their first visit to the ocean. Their excitement and fascination moved me deeply, and reminded me that at least the riches of nature, so abundant in the Bay Area, are available to all at no charge.

The Sacramento River Delta, too, was an accessible destination spot, where water-skiing was a favorite activity. Warm temperatures cooled by lake breezes as we bobbed on the water helped to create peaceful afternoons capped by breathtaking sunsets. State parks from Oregon to the Mexican border made for fun family camp-outs. When we camped at Año Nuevo, near the elephant seals, or at Point Lobos, where we spent our days among the marine wildlife, we felt as though we owned the world. It was not hard to create memorable and meaningful social activities on a limited budget. What a contrast to expensive amusements like Disneyland, which are filled with tension as the youngsters' eyes fill with desire for trinkets and toys while the parents are still reeling from the entrance fees.

Enjoying the natural beauty preserved in state and national parks, wildlife reservations, and protected coastline doesn't cost a lot of money. And to tell the truth, I find it more fun and more relaxing than the expensive amusements that California offers. Whether we brought our own sandwiches or dined in restaurants, the California landscape that is so easily accessible from Silicon Valley was and continues to be ideally suited for leisure activity with families and friends.

At home, the style of entertaining was far-ranging, too, from casual potluck suppers to lavish corporate parties. Each had its purpose in helping to establish long-held friendships and sustaining a community of newcomers.

Our Stanford University faculty friends were perhaps most expert at ultra-casual, inexpensive entertaining, often throwing potluck suppers with Nobel laureates as guests. Their homes—many of them Eichlers with wide-open floor plans—allowed those in the kitchen to participate in animated, often complex intellectual discussions without missing a beat. Most frustrating to me at these gatherings was the habit of the highly intellectual guests to open big questions for consideration and then, suddenly move on to a new topic. It took me a long while to realize what these world-class university professors were doing: rather than providing answers, the best teachers were expert at formulating important questions. It was their life's work, as well as their pleasure, to ponder the various and multifaceted possibilities. Definitive answers, which my work required me to develop for each project, would spoil the fun.

At the other end of the social spectrum, corporate leaders, especially those in hotel, restaurant, and retail businesses, entertained differently. Many of the hosts had connections with sports or movie celebrities, and part of the thrill of these parties was meeting the stars. The hosts' homes were designed for large parties, and because the unusual homes often became the topic of party talk, I was often invited as a conversation piece, to elaborate on the design concepts that lay behind the houses' features.

Bud and Leah Levitas gave me my entrée into this style of entertaining. They gave me the opportunity to design my first major home in 1955. It took a lot of courage for this very successful liquor distributor to run the risk of hiring an unproven young architect to handle a commission on six acres of Portola Valley land. The Levitas property had limitless beauty and distant views. Deer grazed on the meadows looking out over wooded glens. Siting the house and building a residence in harmony with the natural setting was not a job for an amateur. The Levitas's faith opened many doors for me, and I am very grateful to them.

The Levitas's style of entertaining was different from the Stanford faculty's. Rather than passing dishes through a cut-out between the kitchen and the dining room, food was served by a well-dressed couple with Old World charm. Although dress was casual—usually golf attire and a blazer—the fare was not: we dined on abalone puffs, marinated prawns, steak skewers, and wonderful sushi as opposed to the spaghetti or barbecue that was served at the faculty gatherings. The men split off and talked business, sports, and travel. The guests were hotel and restaurant owners and business leaders—prominent people like the Pritzkers and the Swigs in the hotel business, the Mondavis in the wine industry, and major retailers. From the sporting world, Vince Lombardi of the Green Bay Packers, Buck Shaw of the San Francisco 49ers, and Mike McCormick and Hobie Landreth of the San Francisco Giants were regular guests. And everyone wanted to talk about the house. They were fascinated with architecture. The guests were relatively young people of means, and they were all potential clients. Parties like these helped me a great deal in getting my work.

This is the type of entertaining for which Silicon Valley became known, but it represents only a minor portion of the lives and values of most of those who have been successful in Silicon Valley. The day-in and day-out lifestyle actually is a down-to-earth, casual life that includes children. We enjoyed our kids' sports teams and the opportunity to get to know the other parents. School activities created social opportunities. For the most part, we lived in blue jeans, hiked with other families, and lived a low-key lifestyle.

My friend Donald Pritzker, who founded the Hyatt hotel chain, tried to go one step further by emulating hotel-style entertaining in his Atherton home, which featured all the amenities of a hotel, from tennis and swimming to snack bars and shuffleboard. The acreage included master bedrooms and guest suites, flag football space and elegant dining, yet all in the spacious, light, and airy atmosphere of California living. Diplomats, heads of state, and celebrities were regular guests of the Pritzkers, who had taken great pains to blend landscape architecture with the residence, which was designed by my firm and decorated by Eleanor Forbes of Gump's.

The son of a brilliant Chicago businessman and the brother of a child prodigy, Don Pritzker wanted to steer clear of the family business and try to make it on his own merits. After the Korean War, he came home by way of San Francisco and told me, "I don't want to go back to Chicago and sit in that office with my father and my brother. I want to do something on my own."

That "something" turned out to be running the family-owned motel near the old Los Angeles International Airport. The Pritzker family had purchased the run-down motel from a man by the name of Hyatt Van Damme. Don Pritzker liked the name Hyatt, so he named the newly-acquired hotel after the seller. It was small, but it was the only hotel near the airport. With no competition, he could set his own rates—for guest rooms, conference rooms, and catering. It turned out to be a formula for success. With the advent of air travel after World War II and the national expansion of big business, some developers saw the potential for airports as hubs for national and international business meetings. Rather than coordinate and pay for ground transport to a downtown conference room, they thought, why not build the conference centers near the airports? These developers foresaw a time when managers from all over the country would fly into an airport and meet at an adjacent hotel.

The Pritzker family was one of the first to recognize this opportunity. The early Hyatt hotels were two-story, wood frame, motel-style buildings. Construction of a concrete high-rise ran 50 percent higher than a low-rise, and Pritzker had to be prudent. The cost of the building was a big expense to be amortized, one night at a time, by paying guests.

The Pritzkers bought a second hotel near the Seattle-Tacoma International Airport, also calling it Hyatt. Then they bought a third and a fourth, in the Bay Area—one in San Jose and one in Burlingame, near San Francisco International Airport.

The distinctive, atrium-style high-rise hotel for which Hyatt has become famous originated in Georgia. Architect and financier John Portman and a partner built the innovative Peachtree Center in Atlanta, which was a cylinder of guest rooms opening onto indoor landings, with meeting rooms, banquet halls, restaurants, bars, and shops off the lobby. The rooms surrounded a cored-out middle atrium, which was planted with indoor greenery that landscaped the bars, shops, and restaurants on the hotel's main floor. The design was extremely innovative for its time.

Having built his hotel, Portman searched and searched, but could not find any experienced operator to run the hotel for him. At long last, he spoke to Pritzker, who up until this point had run only a handful of low-rise motels. The contract between Portman and the Pritzkers pasted the Hyatt name on the Peachtree Center and gave Pritzker the freedom to manage the hotel as he saw fit. He received a management fee in return. Not only was the deal a smash success, it led Hyatt out of the small motel business and into hotel management in a major way. Soon, large companies like Prudential, General Electric, and Ford Motor Company began to sink some of their fortunes into real estate, erecting huge hotels that Hyatt contracted to run for them. The management contracts were lucrative; additionally, Pritzker had minimal financial exposure. He did not have to put up any money for property acquisition or construction. The arrangement that Pritzker repeatedly reached with hotel developers was a win-win situation that triggered a whole new direction for the Pritzkers and spawned the Hyatt chain as we know it today.

As the Hyatt chain developed, it grew from fly-in airport hotels to a chain that included urban and suburban conference centers and luxury resort properties. The Hyatt Rickey's in Palo Alto was the most active hotel between San Francisco and San Jose. With close ties to Stanford University, the local Hyatt lodged visiting sporting teams, visiting parents, and business gatherings. The Hyatt Rickey's was a variation of an airport hotel, offering well-equipped meeting rooms and a range of guest accommodations, from individual cottages to a high-rise hotel sitting in the middle of a lake. The hotel was reminiscent of the delicate architecture of Venice in a modern, clean, ranch-type setting with views to the distant hills.

Today, only a short while later, the Hyatt Rickey's hotel is undergoing major change to keep up with the area's rapid growth. The entire project will be replaced with much more intense development, including a new high-rise hotel and much-needed housing, which has been mandated by the local community.

My first opportunity to build a new, interesting hotel occurred when the Pritzkers decided to build in Monterey on the site of the old Del Monte Hotel. The architecture of the Hyatt Regency Monterey was influenced by the old hotel, which had been destroyed many years earlier. The new structures spread out in a variety of three-story buildings along the eighteenth fairway of the old Del Monte Golf Course. In the dining room, which overlooked the seventeenth green, drinks and food could be enjoyed on adjacent brick patios at umbrella-covered tables. Beautiful live oaks cast shadows on the patios, setting a relaxed tone. This 300-room project was adjacent to the old Mark Thomas Inn, which the Pritzkers bought and incorporated into the project. There were multiple swimming pools and interesting courtyards. The terrain had a variety of levels. But the real beauty of this project was the magnificence of the trees surrounding the golf course. The building snuggled in among Monterey pines and dense oaks. The combination of redwood buildings with rich brick columns integrated the buildings and the landscaping, creating a timeless environment.

When Pritzker opened the hotel and resort, the party he threw was not to be forgotten. Guests boarded a train on the old Southern Pacific route founded by the Big Four railroad magnates: Leland Stanford, Mark Hopkins, Charles Crocker, and Collis Huntington. The train began its route in San Francisco and traveled south, along the Peninsula, picking up folks along the way. Everyone detrained in Monterey for a weekend of luxury. From the accommodations to the entertainment, the scope and style of the event was unparalleled. Peter Duchin and his orchestra from New York played to a black-tie ballroom full of women in designer gowns and exquisite jewelry; golfers enjoyed a verdant green course in the cool, Monterey mist; we lounged around multiple pools, embraced by the timeless beauty of our surroundings.

Finding ourselves among the guests in Monterey meant we had traveled quite a journey from the humble house we rented in Los Altos when we arrived in California in 1952. That house was in an orchard tract, wedged between apricot trees. There were no curbs or gutters—not even sewers, only septic tanks. Nor was there much traffic. The neighborhood children played together in the street in front of the houses, bringing together families who might otherwise never have met. Our daughter, Joanie, who was then five years old, had a favorite friend from across the street, with whom she would play for hours —inside, outside, at our house, and at theirs. One day, the girls came into our kitchen together, to present a proposal to my wife. The neighbors had recently joined the new Methodist church in Los Altos, and Joanie's friend was enrolling in Sunday school. If we'd like, the neighbor would be happy to enroll Joanie, too, so that the girls could attend Sunday school together.

Joanie was excited. She wanted to go. We liked spending time with this family, and she shared their contagious enthusiasm for the new church. But we were Jewish, and we were not comfortable about where this might lead.

At the time, there were no synagogues or Jewish religious schools in the area. The closest was in San Jose, which, in 1952, was an hour's drive through agricultural farmland. Neither state nor federal freeways had been built at that time. Joanie's enthusiasm for attending Sunday school forced me to consider the kind of community that my family needed. Her desire to join in made me see that I had to get involved. I had to participate with others, creating something where there was nothing, or risk losing my family's Jewish heritage.

We decided to enroll Joanie in the Jewish Sunday school in San Jose, driving the hour each way for the sake of educating her in our family's tradition. There, we met a number of Peninsula families who, like us, were driving the hour to San Jose and back and had begun organizing to start a Peninsula synagogue.

The new congregation, called Beth Am, or House of the People, began by holding its religious school in a private school facility not used on weekends, worshipping in various churches as church schedules permitted, and running the office out of a rented house. After several years of operating in these various locations, the congregation determined that it was ready to buy land and build. I wanted so badly to be selected as the project architect, and to have an opportunity to help shape my own community. I had never prayed before, but I wanted this job so much that I remember praying to God, "Please, if I get this job, I am even willing to have my son become a rabbi." Twenty years later, when my grown son, Tom, called me from Israel to tell me that he had chosen an observant, Orthodox Jewish lifestyle, I thought to myself, "God is calling in his chips."

Once I was hired, I began asking questions about the uses of the proposed synagogue buildings. Typically, a client tells an architect what kind of building is desired, the budget, the size, and the number of rooms necessary to accomplish the client's goals. I wanted to design for the congregation's goals; unfortunately, my good intent was misinterpreted. I treated Beth Am as I would any client, but the volunteer community lacked experience or expertise to realize my questions were standard. I was quite embarrassed when, at one meeting, a congregant publicly stated that if I needed to ask so many questions, I couldn't possibly know what I was doing. He and others thought that, as the professional retained, I would decide what to build. But I needed to know such things as what kinds of programs would take place in these buildings? How much would the membership grow over time, and at what rate? Would there be a library on the campus? How many students would each classroom accommodate, and what activities would the rabbi's office need to accommodate? For example, would a small wedding be held there? Most importantly, could we erect this type of building in this community? In order to answer these questions, a design vision had to emerge that would satisfy both the congregation and the community.

Creating a spiritual feel would be an important element of the design. Some members of the congregation wanted to buy land in Palo Alto, on Middlefield Road or Alma Street, both developed areas closer to where most people were living. But I feared that doing so would put our sacred space in the midst of retail outlets, gas stations, and traffic. I was very happy when the congregation opted instead to buy acreage in the residential Town of Los Altos Hills, even if it was removed from the congregation's population center.

Beth Am was the only nonresidential occupant of Los Altos Hills, and in that regard, we were the first to challenge the town council. Just getting approval to build a nonresidential building on the ten-acre parcel that the congregation had purchased was a project. The council was at first adamant that the town was designed for single-family dwellings only. But we found federal statutes that ensured the rights of religious groups to build houses of worship. As it turned out, however, we did not need to bring in legal arguments, because in the end, we were approved for building, 3-2, in a decision that I think was a case of reverse discrimination. The council did not want to be accused of refusing Jews the right to build a synagogue. Ironically, I think a church would have had a tougher time with approval.

But even with approval, vision, and answers to my questions about how the synagogue would be used, I had to proceed slowly and carefully. The first phase of the project was to build a Sunday school. If I placed the first two classroom buildings at the peak of the property, the high, hilltop spot would not be available when it came time to build the architectural centerpiece, the sanctuary. So the first phase of the project was a secondary building—risky, because it did not demonstrate the dominant theme that was yet to come. But, thinking of our children, we opted to build the classrooms first. The rooms were placed back-to-back in two rows, and by leaving out the wall between the two rows, we created a double room that could be used as temporary worship and meeting room space. Later, when we built a sanctuary, we could erect a dividing wall and convert the space to two classrooms.

Although the board of directors was quick to seize solutions and move forward, I took a lot of criticism for the modesty of the first phase. The school buildings were understated in design and subordinate in location so as not to compete with the future sanctuary, and at the time, they made a minimum statement. But architectural drawing of the future building helped restore the congregation's confidence to continue with me. This is long-term thinking, and it is important that architects, their clients, and others proceed with an eye to the future. So many of today's opinion leaders—politicians and the press, in particular—are short-term in their thinking, choosing immediate rewards at the expense of the long-term health of the enduring community.

I felt strongly about designing my community's house of worship, and I poured my heart and soul into it. I began studying the architecture of early synagogues. Historically, Jews were not permitted to join craftsmen's guilds or develop artistic motifs of their own, so in building their community structures, Jews typically borrowed from the design most prominent in the majority culture. Thus, the Jewish community copied the style of local churches, whether that was the heavy wooden buildings of Poland, the delicate lacey architecture of Venice, or the early Colonial and Renaissance Revival styles prominent in the United States.

In the late 1800s and early 1900s, there was a large Jewish migration from Europe to the United States. When it came to building synagogues, they looked back to the cities that they had come from. Many borrowed variations of the Byzantine dome and its delicate tracery, which was originally used by Christians and later adopted by Muslims. Variations on and adaptations of this style are represented in churches and synagogues throughout the United States, mainly in urban centers. The Islamic detail was particularly appealing and was copied by Jewish communities in many forms, some going so far as to copy even the minarets. I guess neither the architects nor their client synagogues realized that these minarets were Muslim calls to worship!

I read all that I could regarding Jewish styles and places of worship from the Second Temple period through the Middle Ages to the present. But because all of the synagogues I could find to study were built in cities, none of the materials or directions seemed to apply to the synagogue we planned to build in Los Altos Hills. The only insights I gleaned for direction were that the sanctuary should be sited on the high point of a hill, that there should be light in the sanctuary, and that the building should be oriented toward the east, toward Jerusalem.

Beth Am's acreage was pastoral: rolling meadows unfurled toward views of the foothills. There were no other buildings in sight. It seemed important to preserve the serenity of the open meadow, to capitalize on the existing views, and to create soft gardens to complement them.

In reviewing the different styles of architecture that might inspire me, I worked my way backwards through history until I reached the Biblical era, and the image of a tent came to life for me. The tent of meeting could be the architectural style of this synagogue in the rolling hills of Northern California. Through large, plate-glass windows 360 degrees around, one could sit under the calm of the tent-shaped roofline and look out onto the natural beauty of green hills and oak trees, for which the site was selected in the first place. A glass panel at the peak of the roof bathed the people below in light and warmth.

Arcades and green courtyards would link the sanctuary to its supporting elements, the schoolrooms, and the administration building, creating a peaceful campus where one could contemplate the deep thoughts that sacred space —whether redwood grove or beach or house of God—inspires.

Today, the congregation has grown from the estimated 500 families it was built for, to more than 1,200 families, including engineers, scientists, and Silicon Valley leaders. Thinking back on my concerns over my daughter's education, identity, and heritage, I feel proud that this congregation has preserved, for at least another few generations, an anchor and spiritual center for Silicon Valley's Jewish community. It has been particularly satisfying to me to see my son and partner, Robert Steinberg, who was three years old at Beth Am's inception, complete yet another phase of building at Beth Am. In 1999 Robert added a multipurpose community room and several classrooms that coordinate with the existing architecture.

My work on Beth Am helped me to win another design contract for a religious community. The Catholic community of Evergreen, located in southern Silicon Valley, was new, and its residents had to develop their own spiritual center where none had yet been established. Largely as a result of the work I had done at Bellarmine High School some years earlier, I was contacted by the Catholic Diocese about designing several phases of their San Jose facilities, including the diocese office buildings, housing for priests associated with the main church in downtown San Jose, and the St. Francis of Assisi Church itself. As part of the interview process for the church sanctuary, I talked about Beth Am and took the selection committee on a tour of the by then well-established thirty-year-old synagogue. The committee was enthusiastic about the architecture, going so far as to say they would like to lift the main sanctuary, with its open feel and panoramic views, directly from Los Altos Hills to their own San Jose property, which also had magnificent views.

Clergy with an artistic flair and deep knowledge of the sacraments capably provided a design for the religious detail that integrated beautifully with our design for the main chapel and a large gathering hall that incorporated many of the elements the committee admired at Beth Am. Rapid growth in the size of the Catholic community since the early 1990s has led to serious consideration of a school building, which may involve major revisions to the church's master plan. This is another part of an architect's work—to be flexible, to make adjustments, and to have the resulting product be as strong as the original concept.

But it was not only the Catholic population that was multiplying rapidly. A general population explosion has led to an emergency in affordable housing in Silicon Valley. As home prices continue to escalate, it is increasingly difficult to attract essential workers to the area: clergy, teachers, police officers, and firefighters are reluctant to come to Silicon Valley, where a modest salary hardly pays the rent, let alone buys a house.

In the 1950s, land was abundant and inexpensive. That is one of the main reasons I chose to settle on the Peninsula, and one of the main reasons that Silicon Valley was able to develop. While housing had begun to spring up in Palo Alto, Mountain View, Sunnyvale, and Santa Clara, it was minimal within an expansive valley dominated by orchards and row crops and ripe for development. In the fifty years between 1950 and 2000, land prices exploded, from $6,500 per acre in 1950 to $4 million to $5 million per acre in 2000. Since more people have money to buy land than there is land available, the demand for housing is far greater than the supply. The housing shortfall is so serious that Stanford University, the Palo Alto Medical Foundation, and other health centers have had difficulty attracting even doctors to the area.

Stanford has attempted to address these issues with subsidized housing. Industry is moving its production to less expensive communities and looking to transportation to ease the pressure on employees who want to own their own homes in Silicon Valley, where corporate headquarters remain. But the community does not always support the solutions proposed by valley employers.

In an example of social problem-solving, Stanford maintains a faculty housing office, which oversees residential properties on the campus. The university offers a variety of programs to provide somewhat affordable housing for its own faculty and high-ranking staff members. For example, since the university's founding grant prohibits the sale of campus lands, residential lots, on which custom homes can be or have been built, are leased to eligible faculty members for a term of ninety-nine years. Since it is the land that has escalated in value, far more than the structures on it, these campus homes can be purchased at more affordable prices than those in the general marketplace. However, the market is a closed one: campus homes may only be sold to eligible faculty and staff members, who assume a new ninety-nine year lease with the purchase.

Congregation Beth Am, Los Altos Hills, circa 1967

Congregation Beth Am bought land for its future home in Los Altos Hills, adjacent to the City of Los Altos. At that time, the town only permitted development of single-family homes. Not even schools were allowed. Beth Am would be the first exception, and there were serious questions about whether the building would be approved by the town council.

The building had to fit in with the style of the neighboring homes, which was primarily shake roof, wood construction that blended with the hills. It had to have a considerable amount of open space around it to feel compatible with the spacious lots that surrounded the homes in the hills. In general, it had to be a good neighbor.

Our challenge was to integrate a large religious building to the satisfaction of the neighbors while meeting the needs of the congregation.

Historically, Jewish synagogues have adopted the architecture of their locales. The style of synagogues in both European and U.S. cities ranges from Byzantine to Colonial to Gothic and other urban styles. None of these would be appropriate for Beth Am's suburban, almost rural location. We reviewed various other styles that might be more suitable to our site, working back through history to find some form or shape that we could use as the historical basis for the building's architecture. Ultimately, we came up with a simple tent shape.

Instead of creating a tent from fabric, we used shingle shakes. A structural system of 12 columns, representing the 12 tribes of Israel, supports the roof of the main sanctuary. Glass walls take advantage of the views and courtyards and help to create a sensitive, spiritual mood. A skylight at the apex of the tent bathes worshippers in natural light. The congregation was enthusiastic about these ideas.

The carefully planned campus not only satisfied the neighbors and the congregation; it also created a spiritual environment that has worn well with the community for close to fifty years.

In addition, Stanford has built condominiums and apartments for its own empty-nesters and single faculty members. The university also has built rental housing for nurses and other essential workers who could not afford to live in the area unsupplemented. Though these residential development plans represent a noble attempt to create affordable housing, however, they are not without controversy in the community. Some environmental groups consistently oppose Stanford's building plans, especially in the foothills, where local residents enjoy walking, hiking, and biking in the open space. Attempts to legislate limits on Stanford's ability to develop its own land are a regular item on the local political agenda.

While Stanford has displayed long-term vision, Silicon Valley corporations—even the most progressive among them—have been more focused on business development than on the housing prices that have sneaked up on them and restricted their recruiting efforts. Had they foreseen the housing crunch, they might have taken action to protect their employees. Instead, corporate Silicon Valley now looks to transportation as a possible solution to housing its employees. Extending BART, the Bay Area Rapid Transit system, all the way around the bay could help, as relatively affordable land is available south of San Jose. San Jose Mayor Ron Gonzales is shepherding the BART extension effort, which was impeded by developer David Bohannon in 1970. Bohannon had made a large investment in the Hillsdale Mall in San Mateo, and he did not want BART to give his customers the opportunity to travel easily to San Francisco to shop. His efforts to stop BART from being extended south along the Peninsula succeeded. Since that time, land has only increased in value, making it more expensive to encircle the bay, and therefore, less likely and a lower political priority.

One of Gonzales's objectives in extending BART is to be able to offer affordable outlying housing and a way to get to work for people who provide service to the Silicon Valley community, including city workers, teachers, firefighters, and police officers. This is an important undertaking. Others have tried it and failed, but now the timing is better and Gonzales's leadership is stronger. He looks to have the strength and the drive to be successful.

Some cities have instituted separate housing corporations, building subsidized rental units or homes for sale to modest-income families, but for the most part, these efforts have been drop-in-the-bucket solutions. A 100-unit project in Palo Alto or a small housing tract in San Jose, for example, helps far too few. And once the recipients' income surpasses a certain level, they are required to move out. At that point, they are too well off to live in subsidized housing but too poor to afford a market-rate home. Revisiting the limits on density in the foothills and reexamining the use of government-owned land, such as Moffett Field, which was originally purchased by citizens and donated to the government, might lead to more extensive, longer-term solutions.

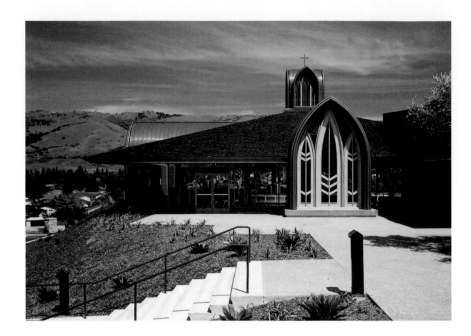

St. Francis of Assisi, circa 1997

After attending a bat mitzvah at Congregation Beth Am, a member of the Catholic community in San Jose approached me to build a chapel for the church. He implied that lifting Beth Am from Los Altos Hills to the church's San Jose site would suit him just fine!

To gain a fuller understanding of the community and its purposes and priorities, I selected a dedicated and religious young Catholic architect as my assistant. We spent two years sitting in on committee meetings and talking with congregants. We brought in a liturgical art specialist. We asked many questions regarding materials, architectural influences, details, phasing, and budget, which resulted in a series of loose sketches. From these, we developed plans for a first phase that would include a chapel and a gathering hall.

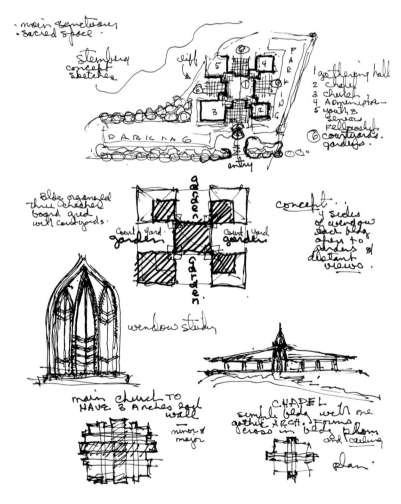

Leontyne Chapel at Bellarmine High
School, circa 1998

While an exhilarating business atmosphere drew people to Silicon Valley, the values of the community are what make them want to stay.

Waves of creative energy—whether radio waves, microwaves, or tidal waves of product development—lured motivated, bright young people to the valley. The risk-tolerant and synergistic industry environment invited them to take a chance on a new idea, to link old ideas in new ways, and to collaborate with other area transplants who found themselves caught up in the creative whirlwind. Is it any surprise, then, that research is more advanced in Silicon Valley than anywhere else in the world?

In these pages, I have described the elements that have crystallized to make Silicon Valley the high-technology center of the world. Cooperation, collaboration, and a free exchange of ideas are no small part of this success. Mutual respect and a willingness to share the glory (or the failure!) has not only telescoped the product development timetable, bringing products to market faster than ever; this creative synergy has brought things to market better than ever. Today, collaboration takes place not only within companies but also across disciplines, linking, for example, a computer scientist and a human biologist to set in motion a worldwide Human Genome Project. Biotechnology companies, pharmaceutical companies, and medical device companies prove that multidisciplinary enterprises improve the quality of our lives. Partnerships are forged every day as support services formerly performed in-house are outsourced and marketing and business services professionals connect clients with like ideas to cross-fertilize them into something new. With so many specialists in the valley—in marketing, in components manufacturing, in business services, for example—the possibilities for collaboration among companies in complementary fields are endless. What really makes these partnerships successful is the appreciation for the background and skills that the other person brings to the table. Whether that person is black, white, yellow, red, or purple makes little difference in a marketplace where ideas are paramount.

This appreciation of difference and respect for the other person's background, a hallmark of university life as well as of Silicon Valley interaction, has found its way into the general Bay Area culture, where diversity is so much a part of the contemporary lexicon that it has become a buzzword. But it is also a reality. Respect and regard for those different from ourselves is a strongly reinforced Silicon Valley value.

We learn from those who are different from us, who bring different skill sets and life experiences to our encounters. In Silicon Valley, getting involved

7

meant the opportunity for self-development as well as development of a community.

Silicon Valley developed because of many factors. Good political leadership was one of them. For example, occupying the North County seat on the Santa Clara County Board of Supervisors was a succession of three dynamic women who worked not because they had to, but because they wanted to make a difference in their communities. My wife, Geraldine "Gerry" Steinberg, was one of those women.

In 1970, Gerry and I lived in Los Altos Hills. On the other side of the range of hills we viewed from our porch sat a major quarry, which had provided cement and stone for many industrial plants during World War II and now provided a major portion of the cement used in Silicon Valley projects. As the quarry expanded, it began to excavate the hills separating it from Mountain View, Los Altos, and Los Altos Hills. At the same time, cities were expanding toward the hills. One calm night, while we were sitting on our peaceful porch, we saw the trees literally shaking on the hills as the roar of quarry machinery hung in the air. If something wasn't done soon, those hills might cave in altogether, revealing a significant eyesore—the quarry. The scene was set for major political conflict.

This is a story of how people get involved to solve problems. Initially, Gerry opposed the quarry with a fury. The quarry had operated since 1933 without restriction of any sort, but Gerry and the other neighbors who felt threatened by it favored putting it out of business. Their emotions ran high as they felt the imposition of an unsightly commercial enterprise encroaching on their pastoral life in the Peninsula foothills.

But as Gerry listened to the neighbors and then organized meetings with quarry officials, she gently, slowly began to move toward compromise. She began to recognize the value of the quarry as well as the quality of life that her neighbors sought in Los Altos Hills and environs. With a level-headed, clear-thinking approach, Gerry, a graduate of Stanford Law School, tried to help the group to identify the issues that concerned them most: for example, the hours of quarry operation, the need for boundaries to protect the hill range, and the establishment of routes that quarry trucks could use to avoid breaking up the residential streets with their voluminous loads. She presented the quarry issues to County Supervisor Victor Calvo, who worked out the details of the regulation program and saw to their passage.

The experience was so successful that when Calvo successfully won his bid for a seat in the State Assembly, the board of supervisors nominated Gerry to fill his vacant seat. Environmentalists supported her because as far as they were concerned, she had saved the hills. Builders and developers supported her because she was fair. She could see all points of view. And she was looking for reasonable solutions.

While many people enter the political fray, just as Gerry did, over an issue that affects them directly, Gerry's nascent political involvement was backed by training, both at Stanford Law School and in the county counsel's office, where she had worked and learned the ropes of county government.

When we arrived in California in 1952, Gerry had already completed her undergraduate degree and had attended two years of law school. Life had interrupted her academic plans: our young family and Gerry's responsibilities at home occupied all her time and attention while I established my architectural practice and set about making a living. Three children and seven years after we came to California, I was happy and productive: I had a beautiful little family and a growing architectural practice. California was all that I had hoped it would be, at least from my point of view. Then, one day, I came home from the office to find my wife crying inconsolably.

"Gerry, what's wrong?" I asked her.

"You're growing and I haven't," she sobbed. "Your architecture is beautiful. You're meeting new and interesting people. You come home radiating with excitement about your work. And here I am, at home with three children. I'm not challenged and I don't know what to do."

"Oh, Gerry, what do you think it would take to stimulate your mind?" I asked her. "Our youngest is in school now. Do you want to go to work?"

Without specialized skills to distinguish her from the pack, she thought it unlikely that she could find challenging, meaningful work. Perhaps more education was her next step.

Stanford University, with a nationally acclaimed law school, was right next door. The question was, could she qualify for admission? We had many friends on the Stanford faculty who volunteered to write letters of recommendation for her. In making our inquiries, we learned that Stanford Law School's first-year class consisted of 125 men and only four women—quite a different situation than today's fifty-fifty balance. This also worked to Gerry's advantage, and she was admitted that very fall.

Admission was the first hurdle. Now Gerry wondered whether she would be able to compete with her bright young classmates. Although she had completed two years of law school at the University of Illinois, Stanford gave her credit for only one. From her perspective, this was a benefit: she had been away from law school for so long that she welcomed the opportunity to repeat prerequisite material that would prepare her for upper-division course work. Gerry kept her nose to the grindstone. Her determination and disciplined study habits were a fine example for our children, who watched as she put in ten- and twelve-hour days in the den with her books spread all around her and her attention focused on the law.

Most Stanford law school graduates went to work for prestigious firms in the private sector. When Gerry graduated, she was concerned that women were not given an equal opportunity in that arena. Stanford promoted public service, and Gerry responded to the call. In the public arena, she thought she would have a better chance to succeed. Contacts established through projects I had done for the county proved helpful as Gerry sought a position in the county counsel's office.

Gerry loved working. She loved the stimulation. The salary was excellent. And the more time she spent working with elected officials, the more she felt that the political arena was an area in which she could have a major influence on building the community. This was far more important to her than money.

Gerry lobbied for a seat on the county planning commission to lay the groundwork for a political career. She gave up her job in the county counsel's office to work on the planning commission for no money. Later, as I mentioned, she was appointed to fill Victor Calvo's vacant seat on the board of supervisors. When that term expired, she ran and was elected to the board in her own right.

After serving for six years, Gerry felt that she had accomplished the goals that she had set out for herself in the areas of land use and the environment. The demands on her time had taken her away from family more than she and I wanted, so she decided not to run for reelection, but to start a business consulting for school districts.

In the 1970s, local school districts were under great financial stress. To raise money, they took to selling off their land, usually in large chunks, to developers who then subdivided it and developed individual lots, which brought them more money than the sale of one large parcel. Gerry had the background and the gumption to tell her clients how they could cut the developers out of the picture and make more money for themselves. She advised the school districts that retained her to rezone their properties for single-family dwellings and to recognize other real estate opportunities. She helped them to develop the property themselves and auction off individual lots to the highest bidders.

An involved, interested, and capable community created an environment hospitable to emerging leaders like Gerry, especially a leader with Gerry's grace and mediation skills. As it turned out, her mediation skills were very important to her tenure on the board: of the five supervisors, two were fairly liberal and two fairly conservative. Very often, it was Gerry's swing vote that decided the outcome of major county issues.

Gerry's main interest was in the area of long-term land use. Her environmental constituents were concerned with foothills development. As their representative, she chaired the county's general plan committee, which ultimately proposed complex new zoning that discouraged development in the hills. Environmentalists were ecstatic, and concessions were made to developers to encourage higher density projects in the flatlands. The builders and business leaders were among the largest donors to the environmental organizations that played such an important role in the quality of life in the area.

The mix of people also contributed to the quality of life in the area. The influence of world cultures, ranging from Cinco de Mayo celebrations to Vietnamese and Thai restaurants, has enriched all of us who have had the opportunity to live in this area.

For example, I remember very well a visit to the Buddhist temple in Mountain View, where my partner Ernest Yamane's young child was participating in a ritual similar to a Christian First Communion. The Buddhist priest in Mountain View was more informal than the priest in the beautiful and traditional Buddhist temple that had been brought to San Jose from Japan years ago. Similarly, in contrast to the exquisite piece of Japanese architecture in San Jose, the Mountain View building's low wood frame was more reminiscent of a 1950s-era Methodist church. Rather than a formal suit and tie, the Mountain View priest wore the casual, comfortable business attire that reminded me of my own Reform rabbi. He talked to the children about Buddha, explaining and asking questions of fifty-some young ones between the ages of three and eight. Each youngster appeared to be fully engaged, one more eager to answer than the next. The children, mostly Japanese, were exceptionally well mannered, and they dressed immaculately. A cuter, more bright-eyed group would be hard to find.

One question that the priest asked stays with me to this day. "Where is Buddha?" he asked the children. One three-year-old pointed out the window. Another pointed to the ceiling. A third patted his own little chest. The children, animated with expectant, Easter-egg-hunt expressions, peeked under their chairs and turned their heads in every direction as they searched out the invisible answer to "Where is Buddha?"

Couldn't the notion that God is everywhere apply in a Jewish, Christian, or Islamic congregation just as well as in this Buddhist temple? This interactive way of teaching was reaching the youngest congregants in a visceral way. Rather than sitting the children in straight-backed Sunday school classroom chairs, the Buddhist priest involved them mind, body, and spirit, creating an unforgettable experience that I still recall with joy.

When this Buddhist priest asked the children, "Is Buddha inside you?" the expressions on their faces and their families' smiling reactions told me that I was learning from a long and beautiful history that provided additional pieces to the puzzle of why Silicon Valley developed in this particular place and time. Involving people in a journey of discovery, whether spiritual or scientific, nets great results. The opportunity to broaden my perspective through exposure to this religious ritual reminded me that diversity—an appreciation for other cultures and other experiences—is an essential element in fertilizing our figurative roots, from the ground up.

At an earlier time in my life, my exposure to Japanese culture was far more onerous. My first exposure to Japanese culture was after my first year of college, in 1942, when I got a job as a junior draftsman at Heart Mountain Relocation Center near Cody, Wyoming. Our three-month job, beginning in June, was to build the barracks for the interned Japanese Americans who were scheduled to arrive at the end of September. The intense fear brought on by the bombing of Pearl Harbor was palpable. I was proud to be working on the barracks that would house the interned, even though it was hardly prize-winning architecture; I, like most Americans, was unaware of the injustice we were committing.

Little did I know when I started my architectural practice in Los Altos in 1952 that my partner's wife had been interned in the very camp that I helped to build. Later, I learned that U.S. Representative Norm Mineta also had been detained in that camp. These were dedicated American citizens—

daughters and sons and wives and mothers and hard-working men who never should have been taken from their homes and who have proven their allegiance to America time and again, before and since the war.

Later, I came to know my two partners' Japanese families as if they were my own. When my partner Richard Tanaka was married in the Buddhist Temple in the 1960s, the affair was not catered, but served by friends and family. How was I to know that I would be called upon, unprepared, to speak at the occasion and to pass appetizers? This was the kind of closeness and informality between people from very different origins that I came to value about life in Silicon Valley.

I ought not to have been surprised to find that Richard and I had many common values and goals. When we began collaborating as partners, we agreed that we did not want to limit our practice to only one type of building. Working on only one type of project had the potential to generate more profit, but we valued creativity and wanted to pursue a wide range of projects, from housing to schools to corporate campuses. We also wanted to be very sure to offer our services to those without a lot of money, such as local governments and nonprofit organizations. Solving social problems architecturally was important to both of us.

When I got involved with designing the new Santa Clara County Children's Shelter, for example, it was not only a job. I, along with county supervisors, fundraisers, neighbors, and generous contractors, created a safe haven for children who were not safe in their own homes. It is incumbent upon us to take care of the less fortunate, whether they are less fortunate financially or emotionally or physically. I am lucky that my profession has allowed me the opportunity to do this.

It is a value of Silicon Valley to protect our heritage as well, and to erect centers of community where activities for toddlers and seniors and foreigners learning English can be conducted in a clean and caring environment. My firm has been privileged to design many community centers, both municipal and nonprofit. Most recently, in 2000, we put the finishing touches on the Los Altos History House, a new structure at the Los Altos Civic Center. Schools, churches, and synagogues are necessary assets in any community that is going to thrive.

Nonprofit organizations and government-funded community assets, including libraries, schools, and museums, depend on the community to help sustain them. In Silicon Valley, volunteer dollars and hours have flowed to them generously, demonstrating a willingness on the part of technology leaders and workers to give of themselves. While the Silicon Valley reputation is financial success, the reality is generosity of spirit. About 83 percent of households in the valley donate to charity. More than half of valley households are involved in volunteerism.

This characteristic value is demonstrated on a corporate level, too. Many valley companies offer corporate matching programs, which match the charitable contributions of their employees, and many have established corporate philanthropy departments, which grant funds to worthy community organizations. Some of the guys with their names on the door have established the wealthiest charitable foundations in the world. The Packard Foundation, based in Los Altos, leads the way. It has funded the construction of Packard Children's Hospital at Stanford and the Monterey Bay Aquarium, provided organizational grants to dozens of nonprofit organizations, and created enormous educational opportunities for children.

Philanthropists have joined together to develop outfits like Joint Venture Silicon Valley, which Rebecca Morgan ran after serving as county supervisor and state senator. Joint Venture is one of several organizations that bring together representatives from business, government, education, and the community to identify and address issues that affect economic vitality and quality of life, including environmental protection, connecting people to opportunities, and keeping local businesses globally competitive. Another such group, Community Impact, established in 1988, offers younger Silicon Valley types the opportunity to contribute their time and effort to done-in-a-day projects, including doing home repairs for senior citizens, clearing park trails, and sorting food bank donations.

And in Silicon Valley, where there are new ways of doing everything, there are new ways of giving, too. The Volunteers Exchange of Santa Clara County stages mock initial public stock offerings to raise cash for charities. In the language of this organization, "stockholders" (contributors) are invited to create "portfolios" of nonprofit organizations that they agree to "invest in" or fund. Another stock-to-services plan is that of Joe Firmage at Intend Change, who uses his share of profits from helping start-up companies through the venture capital process to bolster health, environmental, and youth organizations.

All of these efforts, and many more like them, contribute significantly to the wonderful quality of life in Silicon Valley.

The notion of giving back of the fruits of success to one's community is reinforced at Stanford, where arriving freshman are drafted from their first days on "the Farm" into helping to solicit alumni gifts through telephone appeals. By the time they are seniors four years later, Stanford students are expected to create a class fund themselves, and to give not only their time but also their (anticipated) money to the university that educated them.

In the 1980s, Stanford institutionalized public service as a value that would benefit families, communities, the nation, and the world as much as it would benefit the individual. In 1984, Donald Kennedy, then president of Stanford, inaugurated a Public Service Center (later renamed the Haas Center for Public Service) with a special assistant to the university president appointed as its director. By the year 2000, some 2,500 of Stanford's 6,600 undergraduates were involved in public service while at Stanford. Whether they chose to tutor at-risk youth, work with the homeless, visit the elderly, or explore how governments respond to social issues, students were learning that social responsibility is the mirror image of individual entrepreneurship, and that no community, however large or small, can endure unless initiative and responsibility work in complementary ways. It is a lesson that sticks with many of them.

Quality of life issues have been prominent on Stanford educators' minds from the university's very inception. Stanford's first president, David Starr Jordan, enlisted Timothy Hopkins and ten other leaders from Stanford and Palo Alto to become the founding members of the Sierra Club in 1892. In the hundred years since then, several faculty members have emerged as leaders in the environmental organizations so active in the San Francisco Bay Area. Pulitzer Prize winning author and Stanford Professor of English Wallace Stegner was the first president of the Committee for Green Foothills, which was organized in 1962 to discourage development west of what is now the Foothill Expressway. In 1970 Professor Paul R. Ehrlich, author of *The Population Bomb*; Professor John H. Thomas, well known for establishing Zero Population Growth; U.S. Representative Paul N. "Pete" McCloskey; and Stanford graduate Denis Hayes organized the country's first Earth Day in Washington, D.C., focusing the nation's attention on clean air and water. The late Professor John Gardner was the founder and first president of Common Cause, a nonprofit, nonpartisan citizen's lobbying organization promoting open, honest, and accountable government and eschewing special interests.

In addition, many Stanford faculty members and graduates have served as officials in local, state, and federal governments. The Santa Clara Valley region was blessed from the start with strong political leadership. Just as they did in the areas of business and education, the people who came here wanted to make a difference in the local quality of life. From Santa Clara County through the southern part of San Mateo County, new cities were forming and growing, and the opportunities for involvement were abundant. The unusually high quality of leadership stemmed in large part from a self-starting population that was highly educated and highly interested in the project of building the region that they and their families called home.

From the fields of business, law, education, engineering, and entrepreneurship, there emerged a core of competent, capable people who often stepped up to political posts, perhaps involving themselves first with issues of personal interest, and then advancing to school districts, city councils, and more ambitious seats. Even as the bureaucracies necessarily grew with the influx of people and development, the vast majority of those involved were focused on creating a high quality of life.

Among the most noteworthy, former Stanford President Donald Kennedy was Director of the Food and Drug Administration during the Carter Administration; former Stanford Provost Condoleezza Rice has served as National Security Advisor to both Presidents George Bush and George W. Bush; and Professor of Economics Michael Boskin served President Reagan as chief of his Council of Economic Advisors. Graduates Max Baucus, Jeff Bingamin, Ken Conrad, Alan Cranston, Dianne Feinstein, Mark Hatfield, Tim Wirth, and Ron Wyden have served as United States senators. Three Supreme Court justices are Stanford alumni: Chief Justice William Rehnquist, Justice Sandra Day O'Connor, and Justice Anthony Kennedy. And lest we forget, an alumnus of Stanford's first graduating class, who served his school's football team as equipment manager, was elected to serve his country as president. In 1928, Herbert Hoover became President of the United States.

All of these luminaries represent high achievement. But even more, they stand for service to their community, however broadly they define community. As much as achievement and success are associated with Stanford and with Silicon Valley, this kind of commitment is ours to embrace as part of the valley, too—the part with heart, the part that makes Silicon Valley home.

Though the circumstances surrounding the development of Silicon Valley are rare, they are not irreproducible. Seattle's East Side, for example, was generally considered wilderness until Microsoft came along in the late 1970s. Up until then and for some time thereafter, the locals bused their children east of Seattle to Lake Sammamish, Issaquah, Kirkland, and Redmond for summer outdoor recreation programs, and vacationed there, usually camping. There, as in the Santa Clara Valley, was an abundance of open space available at reasonable prices. There were innovative and industrious individuals seeking to make their mark on the world while building communities that they could comfortably live in. Downtown Seattle, with its attorneys and bankers, retail hub, and

nightlife, was less than an hour's driving distance away. The Seattle Center, erected in 1962 when the city hosted the World's Fair, offered an opera house, a theater, a science center, an amusement park, children's theater, and more: its Space Needle has become the city skyline's signature.

Lake Washington and Lake Union, Puget Sound, and Snoqualmie Pass offered year-round recreation, all within a fifty-mile radius of downtown. The Emerald City, as Seattle has come to be called, offers many fine quality-of-life amenities that have made it attractive to bright young people building a future.

Finally, though not embedded in the East Side community as Stanford University is in Silicon Valley, the proximity of the University of Washington played a major role in the development of greater Seattle's high-tech center.

Additionally, the supplementary strength of regional colleges, universities, and community colleges, such as the University of Puget Sound, Seattle University, and Bellevue Community College, followed the Silicon Valley model. In the Bay Area, San Jose State University, for example, provides more employees to Silicon Valley companies than any other institution. And the University of Santa Clara turns out strong business and law graduates who often stay in the area.

In Seattle, as in Silicon Valley, the mild climate, the natural beauty, the youth and energy of the population, and the presence of a major research university have combined to create conditions in which innovation is likely and high technology has taken off. As has also happened in Silicon

Epilogue

Valley, property has escalated in value, traffic has become a major concern, and essential workers, such as police officers, firefighters, and teachers, are challenged to find housing within the communities in which they work. Traffic snarls are commonplace, complicated by the limits imposed by bridges connecting the East Side suburbs with the city proper.

This snapshot of Seattle underscores that given the right constellation of conditions, "silicon valleys" can be created anywhere. The Seattle experience also illustrates an important lesson learned by Silicon Valley: change is not only necessary, but inevitable.

What will become of the world-famous Silicon Valley? What is the future of a region that is aging, expensive, and land-locked? A region that birthed whole new ways of working, of communicating, of buying and selling? Will Silicon Valley continue to be a hotbed of innovation, or will it ultimately become a retirement playground for the rich and famous?

Though not universal, the predominant values that I have seen demonstrated time and again by Silicon Valley pioneers, entrepreneurs, and philanthropists, as well as plain old folk, leave me with a feeling of optimism and a sense of gratitude for the life I have been privileged to live here. Participating in the development of this region has been the most exciting work I can imagine. When I opened my architectural practice, I made a choice to be a community architect. I did not strive for

national attention. To me, national recognition for a building was not nearly as important as making a contribution to my community. My business grew from good design, good planning, and a solid reputation. Through my career, I was blessed with the opportunities to design churches, hotels, homes, and many public buildings, including community centers, libraries, museums, and courthouses. As a result of my interest in the community—demonstrated both on professional projects and volunteer associations—The Steinberg Group prospered, and I was able pass a thriving business on to my son, Rob Steinberg, who now serves as the firm's chairman of the board.

I am proud of the way that my son has built our practice, bringing to our work an educational background and perspective that I do not have. Rob has recruited talented teams of architects and designers, he has focused on business management to expand the firm, and he has organized the practice in a way that allows us to be involved in more projects than I was able to manage alone. His education in accounting and liberal arts plus architecture has added elements to the business that have helped it to succeed. Combined with the community reputation that he inherited, Rob now finds himself sought after for major regional projects, including the San Jose International Airport expansion and San Jose City Hall. Because we focused locally and

built our reputation in the community, we now find ourselves partnered frequently in major local projects with nationally known architects. This, I must say, is extremely rewarding. But our first allegiance is to our own community, as it always has been. Housing projects at Stanford, local community centers, and schools are important projects that we pursue aggressively.

The success of Silicon Valley is and has been dependent on a team effort. Just as my son and I are different people with different educational backgrounds and different areas of expertise, so Silicon Valley is composed of many intelligent people with different backgrounds and skills. Even within the same educational field, people may have very different approaches to their work, stimulating ideas, intermixing concepts, and coming out at a place that neither would have arrived at alone. This additive process has been essential to the rise of Silicon Valley.

Unlike the superstar system, in which an architect like Frank Lloyd Wright would demand full control of all aspects of a project, from design to heating to interior decoration, the Silicon Valley formula for success has been largely collaborative. Wright worked as an individual, closing the door to others' suggestions; Silicon Valley leaders build teams who work effectively together under a strong captain. This collaboration and cooperation has as much to do with the region's success as do

Early in my career, I was faced with a choice: whether to try to build a national reputation or to focus on my own community. A grueling project in Florida found me flying back and forth almost weekly, exhausting myself to the point that I was unable to enjoy my young family. That was a deciding factor for me, and ever since, I have made my practice one that focuses on building community. To that end, we have engaged in many civic and community projects over the years. Though not the most lucrative, they are most fulfilling.

Los Altos Chamber of Commerce, circa 1962

After World War II, thousands of young GIs with abundant energy poured into the Bay Area, eager to build satisfying and prosperous lives. At that time, Los Altos was a charming bedroom community. In 1952, it was not yet an incorporated city. There were no industries or apartments. All that existed was a friendly residential area with attractive homes located on large lots surrounded by apricot trees. Well-designed schools with large playing fields for soccer and touch football made an important statement. The downtown commercial area, planted throughout with beautiful trees, formed a unique triangle that gave it a personality different from other small cities. It was a town where most any family would like to live, replete with local pet parades, art shows, and community involvement that encouraged lifetime relationships.

With this spirit, the local merchants determined that they needed a chamber of commerce to strengthen retail and lend support to the local business community. The newly organized chamber had no money, so its officers approached a local builder to build the building at cost. He, in turn, asked his subcontractors to assist at cost. In addition, merchant volunteers came forward, supplying materials at cost. I, too, was asked to volunteer my services. In return, I wanted creative license to design a building that would make a statement and have a personality, with no compromise on quality. The merchants agreed.

The city donated a site for this building on one leg of the downtown triangle, where there was an open park with specimen trees. We developed a glass gazebo-like design. The project was a community effort, accomplished with the unusual energy of the post-war GIs. It excited the town's residents. Fifty years later, it is still a modest landmark that evokes a warm response.

History House, Los Altos, circa 2000

Los Altos is my community, so when former Mayor Robert Grimm approached me to design a history museum for our community, I listened. A small group of active leaders who had led some of the valley's most successful companies were behind the project; the City of Los Altos would provide property in the Civic Center; the project would be funded by private money to be raised in the community.

The building would consist of two exhibit halls, a kitchen, gift shop, and administration area. It would serve not only as a museum, but also as a social center where weddings and corporate and private parties could take place. These rentals would help fund the museum's operation.

The committee requested that the building be evocative of the apricot sheds and barns of the early 1900s.

As the architect, I now feel that the most successful part of the project is the three-dimensional space that allows the view of the two exhibit halls and the second-floor balcony. In addition, the high ceiling, the stairway, the placement of windows, the open kitchen, and the way that the lower-floor exhibition hall relates to the patios and grounds all help create a dynamic environment.

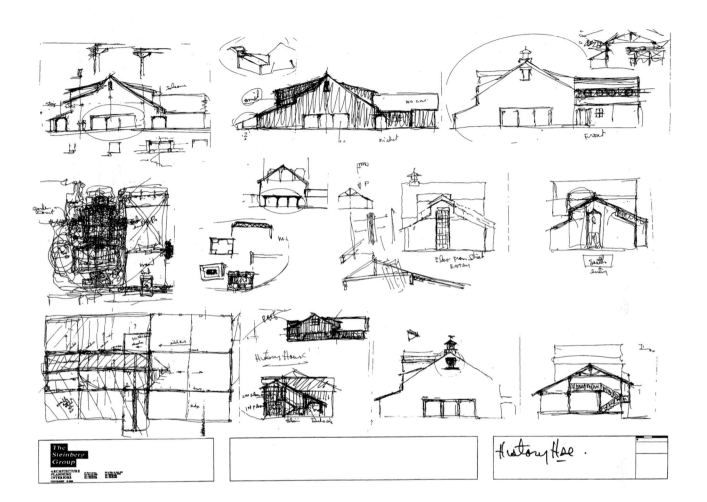

San Ramon Civic Center, circa 1988

Milpitas Civic Center, circa 1982

Cupertino Community Center,
circa 1986

the other factors so important to developing Silicon Valley: the available land, the temperate climate, the innovative spirit of bright, young newcomers, the influence of Stanford University, an involved and intelligent regional government, a population blessed with generosity of spirit.

But besides building the region's business success, collaboration and cooperation also build relationships among peers. When we built Silicon Valley, we built more than corporate headquarters, churches, community centers, courthouses, and homes. We built relationships. It is this aspect—the long-standing friendships, concern for community, and a shared sense of commitment to quality of life issues—that makes the region a place in which I am proud to have raised my family, built a profession, and participated in community life. Whether you call it the Valley of Heart's Delight or Silicon Valley, the Santa Clara Valley is a place that I am proud to call my home.

GOODWIN STEINBERG is a fellow of the American Institute of Architects. Educated at the Illinois Institute of Technology and the University of Illinois, Mr. Steinberg is Chairman of the Board, Emeritus, of The Steinberg Group, a community-oriented architectural firm that has grown to more than 100 associates since he opened it in the Santa Clara Valley when he came west in 1952. Over the last fifty years, Mr. Steinberg has designed a wide range of award-winning projects, from industrial and educational buildings to houses of worship, community and civic centers, and single-family and high-density housing. In *From the Ground Up: Building Silicon Valley*, he offers a unique perspective on the development of the high-technology capital of the world.

SUSAN WOLFE, an award-winning author and community leader, is a graduate of Stanford University and the prestigious Wexner Heritage Foundation seminar in Jewish studies. The author of four previous works, including the acclaimed novel *The Promised Hand*, Ms. Wolfe was born and raised in Seattle. She and her husband live in Palo Alto with their two sons.

In this index **boldface** is used to indicate an illustration.